FLYING STAR

FENG SHUI

— MADE EASY —

ACQUIRE SECRETS OF FORMULA FENG SHUI
GET THE KIND OF RESULTS YOU'VE ALWAYS WANTED

GOODBYE TO MONEY PROBLEMS • FINANCIAL SECURITY
STOP RELATIONSHIP WOES • WEALTH & PROSPERITY
WELLNESS OF HEALTH • **SUCCESS OVER COMPETITION**
BEST EXAM GRADES • STUNNING CAREER ACHIVEMENT
SATISFYING PERSONAL GROWTH • **FRIENDSHIP FORTUNES**
HAPPY CHILDREN LUCK • GREAT ROMANCE & MORE

 **LILLIAN TOO**

Published by KONSEP LAGENDA SDN BHD (223 855)
Kuala Lumpur 59100 Malaysia.
Websites: www.lillian-too.com • www.wofs.com
Email: webmaster@wofs.com

Flying Star Feng Shui Made Easy by Lillian Too
© Konsep Lagenda Sdn Bhd

Editorial Director: Jennifer Too

ISBN   9 7 8 - 9 8 3 - 3 2 6 3 - 9 0 - 5
Published in Malaysia
November 2007

LETTER FROM THE AUTHOR

I f this is the first time you are reading about FLYING STAR FENG SHUI, welcome to a method that could change your life, for within these pages contain many things that once were secrets and the success of feng shui makeovers enjoyed by the Chinese tycoons of Asia was due in large measure to the application of these secrets. In recent years, old texts have surfaced and master practitioners have been more forthcoming in sharing their knowledge. Flying Star has thus now become accessible.

Read this book from start to finish giving yourself a comprehensive overview of the fundamental concepts of compass feng shui. Next, learn the formula, familiarize yourself with the charts, understand the meanings of the numbers and then superimpose the charts and the numbers over your floor plans. This is how you read the energy of your space.

Flying Star is very easy once you understand how it is set up. It is much easier than other methods of feng shui because it is precise and accurate. When you get it right, it works fast, so you will feel encouraged by its results.

Flying Star feng shui addresses the dynamics of energy changes that take place over time and you will discover that the three most important areas of your life – your prosperity luck, your relationships luck and your health luck – will all show vast improvement once you start to practice Flying Star. Success comes more easily and you will attract new opportunities for advancement and happiness. Those already familiar with Flying Star will find this book useful as a comprehensive text that contains all the required references and meanings of numbers with their 81 combinations. This book has been simplified to make a very powerful formula of feng shui easy to learn.

It has been a joy to write this book and I hope it will bring your practice of feng shui to a new and higher level of effectiveness.

1 WHAT IS FLYING STAR FENG SHUI?

Flying Star feng shui is a powerful method that brings fast results. It is formula based and uses the directions of the compass to define lucky and unlucky sectors of a home (or building) during different time periods. There are many different ways to practice feng shui and not everyone uses the compass but probably of all the different methods in use today, the easiest to master, most directly relevant in a modern environment and which bring noticeable results quickest are methods that offer recommendations on the basis of compass directions. The most potent and fastest working of all the compass-based methods is Flying Star feng shui.

There is magic in the uncanny way Flying Star warns of dangers of misfortune, loss, illness and accidents coming and there is great potency in the way it offers ways to activate for wealth, for financial success, for relationships and for recognition luck, as well as many other kinds of good fortune.

Flying Star uses compass directions and time periods to define the flow of positive and negative energy. It is easy to learn and use because it is very specific so in many ways, it is like a scientific tool. But as with all such tools, effort must be applied to ensure accuracy in the measurement of compass directions and correctness in the charting of energy and generating the charts that make up the basis for feng shui investigation. Analysis of the charts and feng shui recommendations follow a specific formula, so the method is precise, requiring not only accuracy in generating the charts but also skill in interpreting them.

Flying Star is scientific and factual and is based more on method than on the feel or intuition of the practitioner. It takes the guesswork out of feng shui practice and offers precise ways of marking out space, protecting space and enhancing space.

It is a very exciting dimension of compass formula feng shui, and because results are usually felt very soon after changes are made, it has become the preferred vehicle for formulating the broad base on which all of one's feng shui recommendations can be based. It is the starting point for making any kind of serious investigation of one's feng shui and for diagnosing all the things wrong with one's feng shui. Often just checking one's Flying Star feng shui is sufficient to find answers to whatever may have been causing bad luck.

What is also great about this method is that for whatever problems may be diagnosed, there are also antidotes or cures. Flying Star offers both the ability to diagnose what is wrong as well as offering the remedies. Flying Star also incorporates a method for analyzing the effect of changing annual and monthly energies that impact on one's feng shui. It therefore suggests not only diagnosis and recommendations on the feng shui of one's space; it also addresses all the things necessary for overcoming bad feng shui caused by the passage of time.

Flying Star feng shui is one of the most powerful ways of creating maximum good luck for the planning and design of homes and work interiors. It is the kind of feng shui that is completely within one's control, unlike landscape feng shui, which is almost always too difficult for the average person to do anything about. Thus while you cannot do anything to change the way mountains and surrounding buildings impact on your home, you can rearrange the allocation and design of the living space inside your home no matter how small your space may be. And this is because in Flying Star you define the space, set the boundaries and are in control of where and how you wish to do your feng shui.

Flying star can be put to good use by anyone prepared to devote effort to understanding its basic concepts and practical applications. All the reader needs is patience and a determination to try and understand the concepts that underlie the formula methods of feng shui, all of which rely on the compass. And while they do not need to use a feng shui Luo Pan, depending instead on an ordinary modern style compass, it is nevertheless useful to know about the Luo Pan about other compass formulas.

This is because Flying Star is in effect the ultimate formula. The best way to learn Flying Star is to get familiar with the compass and to learn the preliminary formulas of feng shui that use the compass before learning Flying Star. This ensures a firm foundation into the basic concepts of compass feng shui, and then Flying Star becomes not only easy to understand but also more exciting to practice.

While knowing about the Luo Pan is useful, an accurate ordinary compass is good enough for practicing Flying Star feng shui.

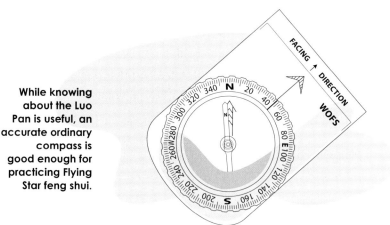

2 THE FENG SHUI COMPASS

The original feng shui compass – also known as a Luo Pan - is at first glance a complex instrument that appears rather challenging. There can be as many as 3000 Chinese characters, numbers, lines and symbolic markings in an average good-sized compass, and the ones used by practicing experts of feng shui are normally at least nine inches in diameter with well over twenty concentric rings of numbers, characters, colours and codes. In truth though, it is just an extension of an ordinary compass.

To old time experts, the Luo Pan is an invaluable tool used as an aid in the practice of feng shui. In ancient times it was regarded with great awe. Against a background of modern computerization technology, the feng shui compass is no longer such an awesome instrument. It is also not difficult to use once you learn what the characters and codes in each of the rings stand for.

Much of the basic information and secrets of the Luo Pan have been extracted and rewritten into easy byte-sized chunks of knowledge, and much of the required and relevant information contained in the Luo Pan is contained in this book. These summarize all the most important charts and information required to access the formulas.

This book simplifies the theoretical explanations that lie behind the numbers and codes of the feng shui compass, especially those that refer to the practice of Flying Star feng shui. All the fundamentals of the Luo Pan are explained in a user-friendly format that makes it within reach of just about anyone prepared to make a serious study of the subject. The markings of a typical Luo Pan contain a wealth of feng shui secrets that have survived the centuries. Feng shui knowledge is believed to have been passed down from masters to disciples for hundreds of generations, and of course, a great deal of the formulas were also written down in texts, and these complement what are summarized in the Luo Pan.

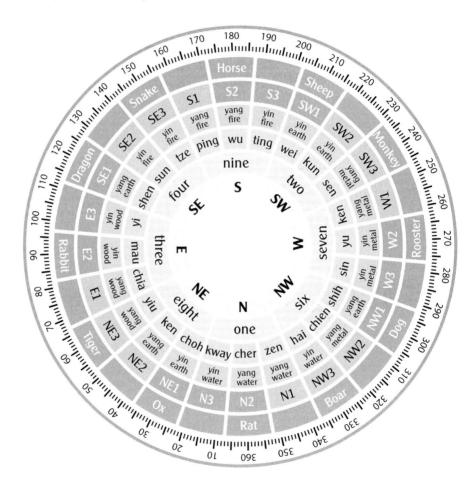

The above shows a simplified Luo Pan. Note the 8 directions and the 24 subdirections which are also known as the 24 mountains. The names of the 24 mountains are also shown in the compass.

3   FORMULAS IN FENG SHUI

The study of feng shui incorporates different methods and commentaries from experts through the centuries. Many of its practical secrets would fill a whole library. So expect there to be some controversy regarding interpretation and applications. With feng shui becoming increasingly popular through books, courses and discussion forums over the Internet, and with China opening up to the world, who knows how much more of feng shui's once secret formulas could explode onto the world's consciousness. It is only a matter of time before feng shui joins the swelling volumes of discoveries labeled quantum physics as more people become enamoured of the theory of chi − the belief that our spaces, bodies and even our lives are influenced and affected by the intangible energy life force known as chi.

In compass feng shui, we take a very technical approach. This may sound as if it is going to be difficult, but actually, taking a technical approach makes the practice of feng shui much easier. Why is this so?

Because when we take a technical approach, we have to be very specific about methods, measurements and dimensions, and about applying the theories and concepts that form the foundation of the practice. This in actual fact removes much of the "instinctive" or "judgmental" dimensions of the practice. It becomes a more precise and exact skill. From this perspective, we can say that feng shui is really very scientific, exact and precise. Get it right and Flying Star feng shui can create truly auspicious energy for you. Get it wrong and it will not do anything for you.

4 MAKING FENG SHUI JUDGMENTS

W here feng shui requires judgment is in determining how to apply and combine different formulas, how to interpret the charts derived from the formulas and how to use them to improve the feng shui of space over different time periods. Sometimes simply determining orientations can be difficult. Not everyone will agree to the "facing" and "sitting" directions of a home, and some of today's modern homes can be challenging in terms of just getting the "facing" direction right. If you try to determine the facing direction of a modular type home, or an apartment building where the ground floor are just car parks with staircases by the sides of the building or elevators taking you to the floors above, then the facing direction is not easily determined. You will need to make a judgment about the facing direction. The "facing" and "sitting" directions of houses and buildings are important because Flying Star is based on these directions. If you get the directions wrong, your analysis will likewise be wrong.

So as you develop familiarity with Flying Star, you are certain to discover that in addition to it being a science, it is also an art; it requires good judgment based on meaningful experience. The more cases you study and the more practical experience you have, the better you will be in developing the feng shui "eye". You also need a keen awareness of surroundings, so you have to take note of physical structures, shapes, symbols, buildings, angles, gardens, roads, rooms and so forth. These structures have an effect on the feng shui of a house and although you may be using Flying Star to undertake the analysis, nevertheless you will still have to respond to how these physical structures affect the way you use Flying Star.

5 USING THE COMPASS

The Luo Pan is exactly the same as any modern compass. It is not a different tool but it has feng shui formulas contained in the concentric rings around the compass placed in the center. The Luo Pan contains condensed feng shui formulas in one carry-all instrument. Information in a Luo Pan can be presented in charts in user-friendly formats and stored in easily retrievable form inside hand-held palm size computers.

So all anyone needs is a simple compass to determine bearings and orientations.

This is what this book contains – all the information of the Luo Pan that pertains to yang dwellings i.e. houses of the living (as opposed to grave sites or houses of the dead). Practical examples are used to explain complex applications but as you go deeper into the subject, you will be amazed how easy Flying Star can be.

Do not expect to become a master overnight. The formulas of feng shui are easy to understand, but if you want depth and potency in your practice, you need to practice as much as possible. Superiority in application comes from practice and experience.

The more you use the formulas, the more profound your use of feng shui will become. Then you will begin to appreciate the genius behind the whole system of environmental science that was used four thousand years ago and which continues to have such relevance today.

6

DETERMINING DIRECTIONS

The first lesson in Flying Star is to understand that all compass directions are relative. Directions do not exist without a reference point. In feng shui, the compass is used to measure the flow of chi currents in and around a piece of property or building. Thus the whole home is the starting point, and from this, the compass is then used to divide the spaces within into directional compartments where chi (or energy) flows. Then the chi of each compartment of space is analyzed.

To delineate sectors that emanate outwards from a central point, you can divide the 360 degrees of any point into eight segments of 45 degrees each. These correspond to the primary and secondary directions – North, South, East and West, and NW, NE, SW and SE.

The 45 degree segments have their corresponding attributes, elements, colors, numbers and meanings. Just knowing the meanings of these eight directions enables any amateur feng shui practitioner to benefit from correct placement of doors, objects, rooms and so forth. Contemporary feng shui is based on this simple method of following the various attributes and symbolic meanings of the different directions, and to arrange and decorate the space in accordance with pre-set guidelines. This is the most basic formulas and requires only for the practitioner to place enhancers that activate the energy of the eight compass sectors. This method of feng shui has been used with great success as it is based on the attributes and eight directions of the Pa Kua.

Symbolic enhancers are auspicious objects that have significant meanings associated with good fortune. Feng shui practice originates from the symbols of trigrams and elements. So using the Pa Kua as a starting point is a basic feng shui method. In this book, we go deeper.

8 ASPIRATIONS PA KUA CHART

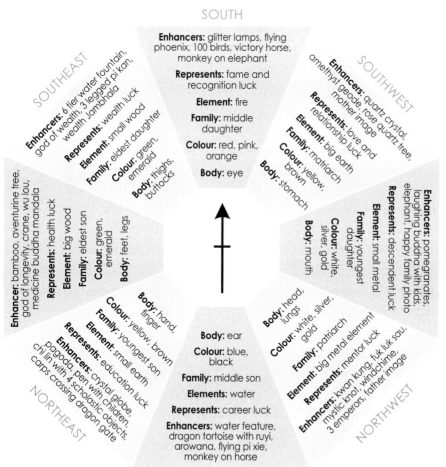

SOUTH

Enhancers: glitter lamps, flying phoenix, 100 birds, victory horse, monkey on elephant

Represents: fame and recognition luck

Element: fire

Family: middle daughter

Colour: red, pink, orange

Body: eye

SOUTHEAST

Enhancers: 6 tier water fountain, god of wealth, 3 legged pi kan, wealth Jambhala

Represents: wealth luck

Element: small wood

Family: eldest daughter

Colour: green, emerald

Body: thighs, buttocks

SOUTHWEST

Enhancers: quartz crystal, amethyst geode, rose quartz tree, mother image

Represents: love and relationship luck

Element: big earth

Family: matriarch

Colour: yellow, brown

Body: stomach

EAST

Enhancer: bamboo, aventurine tree, god of longevity, crane, wu lou, medicine buddha mandala

Represents: health luck

Element: big wood

Family: eldest son

Colour: green, emerald

Body: feet, legs

WEST

Enhancers: pomegranates, laughing buddha with kids, elephant, happy family photo

Represents: descendent luck

Element: small metal

Family: youngest daughter

Colour: white, silver, gold

Body: mouth

NORTHEAST

Enhancers: crystal globe, pagoda, pen with children, chi lin with 4 scholastic objects, carps crossing dragon gate

Represents: education luck

Element: small earth

Family: youngest son

Colour: yellow, brown

Body: hand, finger

NORTHWEST

Enhancers: kwan kung, fuk luk sau, mystic knot, windchime, 3 emperors, father image

Represents: mentor luck

Element: big metal element

Family: patriarch

Colour: white, silver, gold

Body: head, lungs

NORTH

Body: ear

Colour: blue, black

Family: middle son

Elements: water

Represents: career luck

Enhancers: water feature, dragon tortoise with ruyi, arowana, flying pi xie, monkey on horse

7

SUBDIVIDING
THE 8 DIRECTIONS

The eight major directions of a compass - South, North, East and West, and Southwest, Southeast, Northwest and Northeast - can each be subdivided into three subsegments. This fine-tunes compass feng shui into a more subtle division of space. In many of the advanced formulas, the basis for differentiating houses and built-up structures is categorized according to the three sub-segments of the eight main directions. We call these subdirections the 24 mountains of the compass. This means that instead of looking at only eight directions, we now have 24 directions. Three multiplied by eight gives us 24. Each of these subdirections covers an angle of fifteen degrees (360 degrees divided by 24 degrees gives us 15 degrees).

Each of these 24 directions is referred to as a "mountain", so the 24 directions are collectively referred to as the 24 mountains. If you wish to practice compass feng shui, you will find it beneficial indeed if you gain familiarity with the 24 mountains. Each mountain comprises an angle of fifteen degrees, and each angle of direction contains a range of meanings that define the variables of the most powerful formulas of feng shui.

The study of the 24 mountains is central to the cosmic chi being analyzed. (Please refer to the compass on page 10). There are Chinese names given to these 24 mountains, but for the moment, it is not necessary to learn these names. For now, just think of them as subdirections of the main directions, so think of them as South 1, 2 and 3 OR North 1, 2 or 3 and so forth.

8

THREE TYPES
OF NORTH

The Three Harmony Luo Pan recognizes three measurements of North - True North (often indicated by the sundial), Magnetic North and Polaris North. So there are three measurements of North, each of which is 7.5 degrees from Magnetic North in the center. Each North sits on one of three parallel plates. So we have the Heaven plate with the True North, the Earth plate with the Magnetic North, and the Mankind plate with the Polaris North.

In advanced feng shui practice, all three measurements of North are used. Which North we use depends on what aspect of feng shui is being practiced. For feng shui analysis of mountains and rivers and for analysis of time dimension feng shui, different plates and hence different Norths are used. Because of this, the Luo Pan has many rings, each set signifying the meanings and applications of the different plates, and hence the different formulas.

Most formulas for yang dwellings use the Magnetic North of the Earth Plate and this is what we will focus on mostly in this book.

Almost all the formulas relevant to yang feng shui for the houses of the living use Magnetic North of the Earth plate to define North. The Heaven Plate is for undertaking yin feng shui which focuses on the feng shui of cemeteries and graveyards. There is no need to do yin feng shui. Doing feng shui for yang dwellings is good enough to benefit your homes and offices without resorting to yin feng shui.

It is unnecessary (even foolhardy), to dabble with yin feng shui, since this requires practical work in cemeteries. I have a natural aversion to such places, so I have always politely declined offers to teach me yin feng shui.

This book thus has nothing on yin feng shui. The Flying Star formula in this book uses magnetic North, so you can also use an ordinary (but accurate) western-style compass to follow the method indicated in this book.

The environment of present day 21st century is very different from ancient China.

9 TODAY'S ENVIRONMENT IS DIFFERENT

Application of Flying Star in today's environment must take account of how buildings; roads, townships and cities have changed over the centuries. The living environment of the 21st century bears no resemblance to that of ancient China whatsoever. So the circumstances and visual appearance of today's world is not the same as when feng shui first developed, took root and flourished. The chi of the old days was not as complex as it is today. In the old days, electricity and telecommunications were non-existent.

Man-made or man-induced energy flows across the earth have added to the lines of natural energy, so the kind of chi that affects modern homes is very different from that which affected homes and buildings in the past. It is important to keep this in mind when using Flying Star and other compass formula methods.

We need to be sensitive to the new environment when practicing feng shui, especially when considering the significance of modern structures. Thus satellite dishes, water tanks, transmission lines, multi-level roads to name but a few must be taken account of, since their presence does have strong feng shui implications. The compass can also be used to gauge the influence of neighbouring buildings and structures. To undertake this analysis, you need to determine the sitting direction of your house, finetuning it to a 24 mountains subdirection. Next, check the Mankind Plate Compass to determine the "sitting" element of your house. The feng shui effect of any building is determined by its "element" in relation to your sitting element. If it "produces" your element the building is favourable. If it destroys and exhausts your element, the building is harmful.

When this is determined, reasonable care should be taken to diffuse hostile chi emanating from a nearby building, and to enhance benevolent chi being sent from a beneficial building.

Here the formula uses the Mankind Plate set of 24 mountains and their corresponding elements to study the meanings of nearby buildings, mountains and structures. This is illustrated below.

Note the element of the 24 mountains subdirections in this Mankind Plate Compass. Example: If your house sits NW2, its sitting element is wood. A building in SE3 direction with water element benefits your house, while a building in SE1 with metal element is harmful to your house.

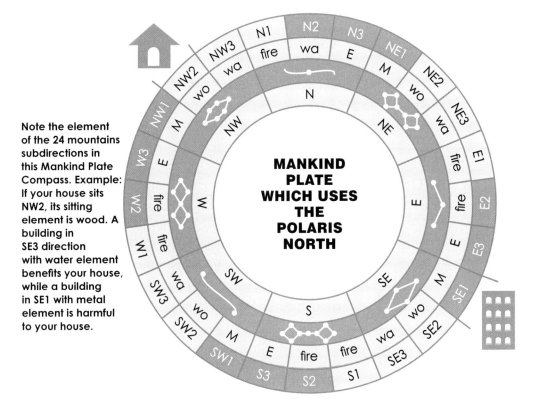

10 GOOD & BAD FENG SHUI

Compass feng shui gives us the key to unlock a veritable treasure trove of different methods we can use to make subtle changes that bring big transformations in luck. Good feng shui always means being protected from premature accidents and death. It ensures your family and all the residents of your household are successful, safe, secure and happy. Living within the embrace of protective chi helps you avert accidents and overcome life obstacles. There is harmony in the home.

Maintaining good feng shui involves taking account of time changes that affect the flow of energy, so monthly and annual afflictions that bring danger are taken care of. Good feng shui must be maintained with regular annual updates. This usually involves the reenergizing of chi, and the arrangement of remedies and placement of enhancers according to the feng shui charts that change from year to year. The annual updating process goes a long way in ensuring residents do not succumb to feng shui afflictions or fall victim to unlucky accumulations of chi, what the Chinese refer to as the "ill winds" that blow from year to year in certain sectors of the home.

Good feng shui often results from well-positioned enhancers placed on the basis of annual feng shui charts. Good feng shui manifests as longevity and good health, success without obstacles, growth in wealth and maintenance of good relationships amongst friends, peers and family members.

11   READING THE INVISIBLE CHI

Feng shui assessment is about reading invisible chi patterns that influence a property or built-up structure. This can be a home, factory, shopping area or office building. These patterns can be determined onsite by an experienced practitioner, but they can also be analyzed by means of special charts generated according to the formulas of feng shui. In the atmosphere of any place, there is always a vibration you can tune into. You can pick up these vibrations if you are sensitive to the environment, but using the compass to demarcate directions and the formulas to generate the charts is a faster and easier way to practice feng shui.

In addition to the importance of the formula and method however is a mind. One's attitude when doing feng shui must encompass the earth and the sky, land and water, yin and yang, productive and destructive forces. So a solid knowledge of formulas and interpretations is supplemented by a wide and open-minded attitude of positive expectations. The practitioner can pick up the vibes of the atmosphere, so always factor in and trust your own instincts as well.

The living universe is a multiple blend of a billion permutations. No two houses or properties are ever exactly alike, just as no single abode has constantly good or constantly bad feng shui. The nature of energy is that it is always changing and always evolving. So when using the compass and the formula of flying star feng shui, it is a good idea to take directions not once, but several times. This ensures accuracy in reading directions.

Chi can be elusive. Chi is not easy to pin down, so taking directions can be frustrating when the needle in the compass refuses to settle down. Be patient. Chi is like mercury, hard to grasp. One can study it, analyze it, live with it, embrace it, feed it, trap it, accumulate it - but it is foolhardy to take it for granted. So be patient and take your directions carefully from different angles. The key is to get the orientations of your home done correctly and then compass feng shui will amaze with fabulous and quick results.

There is a depth to feng shui that is very challenging.

There are those who use instinct or some special metaphysical capability in their practice of feng shui. Others use assessment of physical shapes and structures. Many practitioners use a combination of different personal styles and methods. I have seen a multitude of approaches used by different people with varying degrees of success.

My perspective of feng shui is taken from the viewpoint of a user. I used feng shui extensively, broadly and boldly in my work, business and personal life. Feng shui gave me the competitive edge. For over thirty years, feng shui has been a dependable ally. And while I have experimented with different formulas, performed various rituals, and applied symbolic feng shui in every aspect of my life, underlying all those has been my total reliance on the compass and on Flying Star feng shui. So my starting point is always to check the orientations of any place whose feng shui I am investigating.

12

FLYING STAR & OTHER METHODS

I discovered Flying Star feng shui very early in my practice and these many years using it has made me very confident of its effectiveness. It really does work. The way we orientate and place everything - our beds and tables, how we design our rooms and where we place our important furniture, how we position the main door and how we orientate the house itself - all as directed by the Flying Star energy of the compass directions and sectors - these were such precious secrets when I first learnt them and attempted to grasp their essence.

Eventually I came to know it so well because I saw and benefited from its wonderful results. Flying Star feng shui works such stunning magic, especially when you do it right. Flying Star feng shui has never let me down. And like everything else, using it so often I now practice it like it is second nature to me. It has become part and parcel of my life.

Which numbers to focus on, which room to activate, which star to place more emphasis on, and what direction to use, where to place the main door and a host of many other questions now come easily to me whenever I investigate someone's feng shui. The most wonderful thing about Flying Star is that even though it is a formula, there are always options that force the practitioner to think carefully when choosing between alternative ways of enhancing their feng shui.

In my experience, Flying Star works best when practiced in conjunction with Symbolic Feng Shui because then the two methods bring truly fast and positive results. It is even better to combine Flying Star with the Eight Mansions KUA formula especially in the arrangement and selection of rooms for different members of the family.

In today's world, many of us really only have control over the interiors of our abodes. Those who have gardens do have some control over immediate exterior surroundings, although even this has limitations imposed by city regulations.

But both Flying Star and Eight Mansions which use directions, offer easy ways for interior space to be manipulated to capture the best feng shui.

Flying Star evaluates a property from the perspectives of time periods, while Eight Mansions adds the personal dimension, since this formula takes a personalized approach to lucky and unlucky directions, so it is useful to learn this latter method also. This then enables you to add a personalized dimension to the practice of Flying Star.

13

FLYING STAR MOST POWERFUL

Experts acknowledge Flying Star to be the most powerful system of feng shui. However, because of its potency and its reliance on number analysis, it can at first seem daunting. It incorporates the study of numerology, the powerful effect of the five elements, the two Pa Kua arrangements of trigrams and some previously well-kept secrets of the feng shui compass.

In reality, Flying Star becomes easy once you understand the fundamentals underlying it. Flying Star is easy to learn but harder to master. It requires effort and concentration. However, when you build or renovate your own house, you will seldom go far wrong. Flying Star works fast in making your space feel more embracing and harmonious. It brings an easier life of abundance. But there is the dimension of time changes that must always be factored into the practice. This is the challenge of Flying Star - it is a dynamic practice.

When done right, Flying Star ensures fewer obstacles in your life. There is a method within this formula, that creates a better environment for relationships to become more fulfilling, attracts greater harmony that leads to success, higher incomes and improved wealth luck. Flying Star leaves less room for mistakes. The techniques are specific, and it takes the guesswork out of feng shui.

14   EIGHT MANSIONS FENG SHUI

This personalized method is about lucky and unlucky directions based on a person's gender and lunar year of birth. The date of birth is required to ensure that the changeover to lunar calendar is correctly calculated. Eight Mansions is simple to learn, so easy that even children can use it to benefit them to get better grades and enjoy good examination and study luck. But knowing how to expand the theory into different applications is a little more challenging.

Eight Mansions has many uses. It is at its best when used in conjunction with Flying Star. Both methods use compass directions to define space, but where Flying Star focuses on the chi of the space for the benefit of everyone living within the same residence, Eight Mansions takes a personalized approach.

Both methods look at the orientation of the space being investigated, so using the two formulas together means you are combining two powerful methods. It can be practiced on its own – indeed if you are a total beginner reading about feng shui for the first time, then if all you do is carry a compass and start to sit, talk and work facing one of your auspicious directions based on Eight Mansions formula, you will definitely start to experience an immediate difference in your luck. So if you wish to check on your personalized feng shui immediately, go straight to the Eight Mansions formula and its accompanying table of directions before going deeper into the study of Flying Star.

15 INVEST IN A COMPASS

An amateur practitioner does not need the full and complete feng shui Luo Pan. A Luo Pan is not necessary unless you are planning to become a professional feng shui consultant. If you do decide to invest in a Luo Pan, you should learn how to use it thoroughly and then it becomes an amazing and fascinating tool.

But do not buy a Luo Pan from someone you do not know. In fact, the only person you should buy a Luo Pan from is someone who is teaching you feng shui. The Luo Pans you get in tourist shops are for decorative purposes only. Some say that placing a decorative Luo Pan in the house will cause you to automatically have good feng shui. I am a little reluctant to endorse such a view, but have to admit that this point of view does have its supporters.

When you get a Luo pan and there is someone teaching you how to use it, then it becomes a worthwhile investment. Most of the key information in this book for instance can be contained in a Luo Pan. For the average practitioner of feng shui however, any properly manufactured compass that can measure directions accurately can be used. You do need a good compass to be reliable. Just imagine doing feng shui based on faulty directions – everything done will then be based on a mistake.

So, to get started, you need a good reliable compass. You might find it useful to get a compass with the 24 subdirections marked in as these directions are required in the practice of Flying Star feng shui.

16 ESSENCE OF FLYING STAR FENG SHUI

Flying Star feng shui comprises formulas and secrets that enable the serious practitioner to create excellent feng shui from just taking the direction of any building or property. This method teaches you to make a diagnosis of the property's feng shui through the use of specially generated charts. Homes are marked into compass sectors and the sectors that are afflicted with potentially dangerous "stars" immediately become obvious. Everything is interpreted from the Flying Star charts that are generated based on the compass facing and sitting directions of the house.

Flying Star feng shui is based on the concept that all spatial energy can be expressed in terms of numbers within designated compass sectors. It defines space according to the different afflictions and good luck stars the space plays host to.

The Flying Star chart identifies different kinds of energy afflictions, which take different forms under a whole mélange of circumstances and orientations. Afflictions can be due to (or magnified by) physical structures within the vicinity of the landscape. Or they can be caused by the orientation or placement of the building's doors and entrances, OR they can be simply afflicted by energy changes that take place over time. All these and more can be decoded from a comprehensive analysis of space which is charted using the specific method of generating the charts.

In many old Luo Pans, the Flying Star formula is incorporated into the rings around the compass, but to the layman, the information on these rings is coded and not immediately accessible. There is a however a colourful Chinese legend about the beautiful Goddess known as the Lady of the Nine Heavens.

According to this legend, this divine Goddess gave the Luo Pan to the Yellow Emperor and revealed to him the wisdom and secrets of the feng shui formulas. Using the compass and the good feng shui it provided, the Yellow Emperor succeeded in defeating his enemies, and ultimately in unifying China.

In the ensuing centuries, the compass was progressively enhanced, especially during the period of the Chou Dynasty. During that period, the Duke of Chou followed by King Wen and his grandson progressively combined the knowledge of the compass with that of the I Ching, and in the process established concepts of worldly and divine clairvoyance.

Thus was formulated what would eventually become the fundamental underpinnings of Flying Star and its many related branches. These were regarded as a combination of all the knowledge of heaven and earth. We are thus lucky that as a method of feng shui, Flying Star has survived intact through the centuries and we are able to use it create some spectacular feng shui magic.

THE FENG SHUI LUO PAN

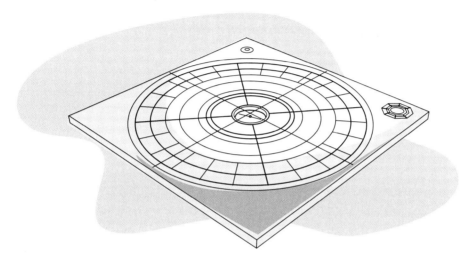

The Feng Shui Luo Pan is first and foremost a compass for measuring directions. So its most important part is the magnetic needle in the center. It is advisable not to compromise on the quality of this central needle since accurate compass reading is vital in practicing Flying Star feng shui.

The Luo Pan divides directions into 360 degrees around a point of reference. This is divided into 8 main directions and 24 subdirections. These subdirections are referred to as the 24 mountains, and each mountain measures 15 degrees. The ring that indicates the 24 mountains is very important because feng shui formulas use the 24 mountains to categorize different types of houses.

Luo Pans should have the 24 directions indicated in one of the rings.

The rings in the Luo Pans contain different formulas, and even when they contain the same formulas they may be presented in a different way, so to the uninitiated, the Luo Pan's numbers and characters can remain in doubt until the rings are explained and interpreted for you! Luo pans are best purchased from a bona fide feng shui master.

Good Luo Pans are made with precision and care. The best are crafted from expensive oil wood that can last for a hundred years. Cheaper substitutes are acceptable, but Luo Pans should never be made of plastic, cardboard or paper. The face of the compass where the rings are placed sits on a base made of wood known as the earth plate. The face of the Luo Pan is usually made of stamped copper plate and in a good Luo Pan, this plate is well stamped and well made.

I want to stress that you do not need to invest in a Luo Pan to become an excellent feng shui practitioner. It is important only to know how to use a compass to measure directions. As long as you have a compass, any compass, you can apply all the formulas of feng shui. In case you wish to invest in a Luo Pan however, do take note that high quality Luo Pans have clear, sharp and well-crafted characters and measurement degrees, and they never rust. So if you are considering buying a Luo Pan, you should make sure it is made of good material and the compass in the center is accurate and of good quality. Choose a size you are comfortable with. A medium-sized Luo Pan usually contains all essential information. Store your Luo Pan with care keeping it away from electrical and metallic devices so the needle stays sound always.

18   BUYING A LUO PAN

f you are fascinated by the Luo Pan and wish to purchase one for whatever reason, here are useful tips worth bearing in mind...

1. Take note of needle quality. This is the most important part of the compass, and the most expensive. The needle should align accurately on top of the red line in the center of the compass. Never buy a Luo Pan with a cheap needle. Remember it is sensitive to metallic objects, so a larger needle might be better than a smaller one.

2. The two red dots must be present and these should point North (the Rat direction) while the point of the needle should point South (the Horse direction).

3. Take note of the "face" or heaven dial. It must be clear and not blurred so that characters can be read easily.

4. Turn the Luo Pan on its earth base - it should be tight but move freely and smoothly.

5. The earth base should be square, to facilitate taking directions by pressing it parallel to a wall or door.

6. It should have a water gauge to ensure the Luo Pan is square to the ground.

7. Finally, there should be a booklet with detailed instructions on each ring of the Luo Pan.

UNLUCKY LINES
ON A LUO PAN

There are special directions that indicate harmful chi and these inauspicious directions lines are shown on a Luo Pan. These lines are described as the cardinal death lines and the major and minor emptiness lines. One of the most well kept secrets of compass feng shui previously known only to lineage masters is that the facing directions of doors and entrances should never lie exactly on the cardinal lines that indicate the exact cardinal and secondary directions of the compass.

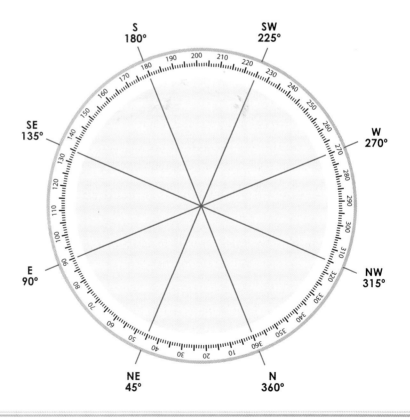

There are eight death lines and these are the lines that are bearing exactly North, South, East and West as well as NW, SW, NE and SE. Here death lines do not necessarily mean death in a physical sense. It usually refers to loss, failure and other extreme forms of bad luck.

On a Luo Pan, these lines are easily identifiable. Thus if North is deemed to be the best direction for you under the Eight Mansions formula and you wish to have your door face North, then you should make sure not to face exactly North, but rather to face a couple of degrees off the exact North. This is true of all the four primary directions and the four secondary directions.

There are also *kung mang* or emptiness lines that spell misfortune and severe bad luck. In all, there are 8 major emptiness lines and these are the lines that separate each of the eight main direction sectors − N, S, E, W, NW, NE, SW and SE − as well as 16 minor emptiness lines and these are the lines that separate the 24 mountain subsectors in each of the 8 sectors.

To know how you can identify these inauspicious and dangerous lines of directions, take note of them expressed as directions here.

Firstly, the death lines are the cardinal directions bearing 90, 180, 270 and 0/360 degrees as well as the secondary directions bearing 45, 135, 225 and 315 degrees.

Major Emptiness lines are directions bearing 22.5, 67.5, 112.5, 157.5, 202.5, 247.5, 292.5 and 337.5 degrees.

Minor Emptiness lines are directions bearing 7.5, 11.25, 33.75, 37.5, 45, 52.5, 56.25, 78.75, 82.5, 97.5, 101.25, 123.75, 127.5, 142.5, 146.25, 168.75, 172.5, 187.5, 191.25, 213.75, 217.5, 232.5, 236.25, 258.75, 262.5, 277.5, 281.25, 303.75, 307.5, 322.5, 326.25, 348.75 and 352.5 degrees.

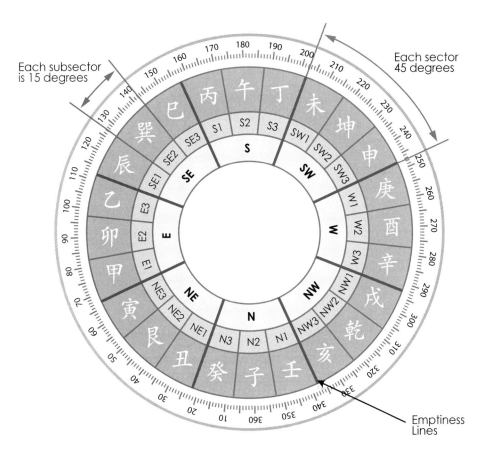

Each subsector is 15 degrees

Each sector 45 degrees

Emptiness Lines

The "Emptiness Lines" are lines that separate the directions. Lines that separate each of the eight major directions are major emptiness lines, while those that separate the 24 mountains are minor emptiness lines. Death lines are the lines that face exactly North, South, East and West.

20 EMPTINESS & DEATH LINES

These are the lines that separate the directions. Note the emptiness lines from the illustration on the proceeding page. If you find that your house or main door is facing a death line, or if it is facing a major or minor emptiness line, and you are unable to change the orientation of your house or door, one method of reducing the negative effect is to place some kind of metal decoration on the door itself. This can be a door knocker (the best are lion head brass door knockers) or you can hang sword coins on the inside of the door.

The introduction of a bit of metal is usually sufficient to change the direction of incoming chi energy so that the main door into the house no longer faces the death or emptiness line. Having said this, please note that if you are having a spate of enormous bad luck and you discover that the door is facing one of these lines, then it might be a good idea to adjust the door slightly so that it no longer faces the dangerous line of direction.

Another little known method of overcoming the threat of emptiness lines is to transform your house into a heavenly abode by placing an altar directly in front of the entrance door. You will find that the Chinese like to place their altars this way and this is an excellent antidote for overcoming the affliction caused by facing a *kung mang* or emptiness line. This not only deflects the ill effects of emptiness lines but also causes the direction to then bring in auspicious luck. Irrespective of your religion, it is said that once you introduce an altar, any kind of altar, the emptiness line gets broken and transformed into an auspicious line.

21

YIN GAPS

In addition to afflicted direction lines, there are certain directions called Yin Gaps, and these are directions that bring stagnation luck. If your door faces any of these yin gaps, they indicate problems in the area of human relations for the residents. Doors that face yin gaps cause problems between spouses and create family disharmony, marriage problems and can even lead to eventual breakups. The yin gaps are the direct centerlines of each of the 24 subdirection sectors.

It is always advisable to ensure that the house itself and its main door do not face any of the death lines, emptiness lines or yin gaps. These are directions that bring secret afflictions. Experienced masters always check this aspect of the feng shui before doing anything else. When advising on the design of new homes, this should always be taken account of. Usually, compass directions are taken during actual construction to ensure that directions are properly read before piles are sunk into the ground.

In China, popular door decorations such as metal studs and doorknockers have the effect of tilting the direction a couple of degrees. This is one of the "secret" ways of avoiding afflicted lines since metal energy affects the directional chi near the entrance into the home. However, since the compass is affected by the presence of metal, it is important to remember that main doors are best made of solid wood. If there is metal placed on the door, these should be factored into account when designating the door direction during construction stage.

PRINCIPLES OF YIN AND YANG

The Chinese have long believed that the creative process goes from one extreme to another, manifesting in endless cycles. The two extremes of fundamental reality are generally expressed as motion (Yang) and quiet (Yin). When either yin or yang reaches its limit, it becomes the other. So from quiet there is motion, and from motion there is quiet. Yin and yang play a big role in determining the quality of spatial feng shui and understanding it is incredibly helpful.

From the classical texts we extract fundamental wisdom about yin and yang forces. Thus it is written that from the cycle of limits where yin and yang continuously transform, one into the other, stem the SIX energies, and from the SIX energies there appear the FIVE elements, and then from the FIVE elements there come the Ten Thousand things, which in essence is everything in the Universe.

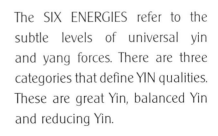

The SIX ENERGIES refer to the subtle levels of universal yin and yang forces. There are three categories that define YIN qualities. These are great Yin, balanced Yin and reducing Yin.

Similarly, Yang energy can also be classified as great Yang, bright Yang and diminished Yang.

The FIVE ELEMENTS express the five manifestations of energy. The Chinese term for energy is chi. The five types of chi are fire, earth, metal, water and wood. They each have a productive, weakening or destructive relationship with one of the other elements, thereby intrinsic in each element are forces that relate it to the other elements. Each element has a Yin as well as a Yang aspect.

The Ten Thousand Things are all the things that make up the material and physical world. The forces of Yin and Yang express the manifest Universe from ultimate nothingness to the material Ten Thousand Things. One becomes two. Motion becomes quiet. Yang becomes Yin. And vice versa. This creative process can be illustrated in sequential order, as shown. This is the origin of trigrams and hexagrams of the I Ching.

Yang is described as the vibration, pulse and movement of the Universe - energy rotating, moving and vibrating at different rates. All of this motion takes place against a background of varying manifestations of yin.

Yin is silence, stillness, non-movement and quiet. The key to understanding yin and yang is to realize that one cannot exist to the exclusion of the other, and that one gives rise to the understanding and manifestation of the other.

Yin and yang are interdependent concepts relative to each other. There is simply no yang without yin, and no yin without yang. Both must be present, otherwise there is absolutely nothing. If you remember this concept alone, you will never forget about balance and how important this concept is to the feng shui of space. Your practice will definitely be improved when balance of yin and yang are factored into the equation of space. Your interpretation of the five elements, their cycles and their meanings will also be enhanced.

23 EVERYTHING IS RELATIVE

When you understand yin and yang concepts, you will understand the theory of relativity and its aggregates. It then becomes easier to understand that everything in the universe exists as interdependent aggregates. Nothing exists of its own accord. When there are no aggregates, things simply cease to exist. It is impossible to completely obliterate either yin or yang, since this will cause both to become nothing!

Yin is said to be denser, less energetic and more material. Yang is lighter, more energetic and less dense. In the interplay of yin and yang, there are a zillion manifestations and variations. The two forces are primordial and everything on earth is an expression of this interaction between the two forces. Despite this however, Earth is regarded as all yin and Heaven as all yang. But the things in Heaven are regarded as both yin and yang when compared to each other. It is the same with all the things of the Earth, which can be either yin or yang, and yet when compared with Heaven, things of the Earth are all yin.

The correct appreciation of these two supposedly opposing forces is what gives practitioners of feng shui, Taoism, martial arts and other esoteric practices the real potential to make progress in their practice.

In feng shui, a genuine understanding of yin and yang forces within any environment is often sufficient to cause good levels of energy to be created. It is the same with the practice of Taoist meditation and difficult physical exercises that raise the fire of inner chi. When one understands how yin and yang energy flows within the human body, one becomes exceedingly healthy. And when one understands their flows in the environment, one can arrange things to enjoy exceptional good fortune. Meditation based on a good appreciation of yin and yang also creates fertile ground for perfect understanding to grow (referred to as divine realizations by religious meditators).

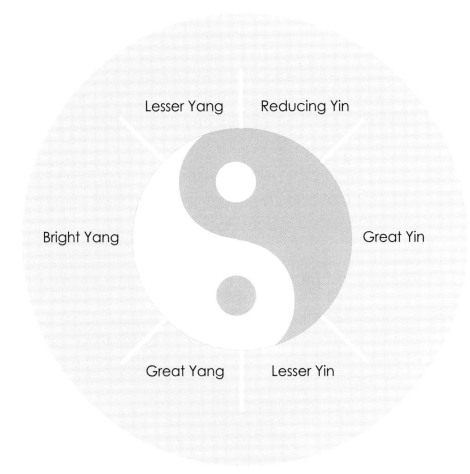

Yin and Yang are the two primodial opposing forces that complement each other. In yang there is yin, and in yin there is yang. Understanding this is the cornerstone of feng shui and this is because the interaction of yin and yang is what gives rise to the six types of energies.

24　PHILOSOPHY OF YIN AND YANG

Yin and yang cosmology also suggests that ideas precede manifest reality. Nothing exists without it first having been conceived in the mind. So the idea of motion precedes actual motion, just as the idea of quiet precedes actual quiet. The idea comes from the mind, so it is the mind that moves energy. Meanwhile, the power of the mind is both relative and absolute.

It is the mind that makes all things happen. Energy moves the body and galvanizes it into action. Energy is the manifestation of the intangible forces of the world and this can have either a yin or yang aspect. At a practical level, the appreciation of yin and yang begins with the ability to know what is yin and what is yang, then from that to appreciate what is deemed to be perfect balance between the two. Here is where the mind has a potent influence on understanding yin yang balance.

Identification at the gross levels is usually not difficult. This refers to knowing that sunlight, bright colours, noise, motion, action, heat, dynamic and so forth are manifestations of yang; and moonlight, stillness, darkness, cold, death and quiet are manifestations of yin.

What is more difficult to ascertain are the subtle levels of yin and yang, or knowing the precise moment when yin transforms into yang and vice versa. It is also difficult to know when perfect balance of the whole has been ascertained. So in esoteric arts, getting the "balance" right is something that comes with experience and plenty of practice.

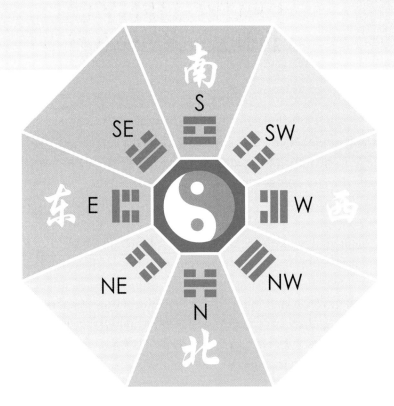

The Pa Kua above reveals the Yin and Yang "face" of the East and West group directions. Thus the East directions North, South, Southeast and East have three directions next to each other and North on its own. It is the same with the West group directions where Southwest, West and Northwest are side by side and Northeast is by itself. This reveals the Yin in Yang and Yang in Yin dimension of the Pa Kua directions.

Allow your instincts to guide you. Do not expect to get everything right immediately. Over time, you will start to develop a sensitivity to the yin and yang of your environment. But you should be relaxed about this. The idea is to acknowledge the power of your mind and your own sensitivity.

25 SYMBOLISM OF THE TRIGRAMS

Trigrams are symbolic representations of how yin and yang interacts, and they are believed to reflect varying densities of energy. They offer important meanings to feng shui practice. The energies of the trigrams are characterized as four sets of two line images described as old and young yang, and old and young yin. Then by adding a yin and yang line above the two line images, eight trigrams are created. These eight trigrams have three lines each. When they are combined with each other they become the six lined symbols known as the 64 hexagrams.

The eight trigrams feature very prominently in formula feng shui; thus, like the I Ching, they originate from the two primordial energies of yin and yang. When you understand the role of yin and yang in feng shui, you will understand the essence of feng shui.

HEXAGRAMS are six lined symbols that comprise two trigrams one above the other. There are altogether 64 hexagrams. These feature in the formulas on YIN feng shui, the feng shui of burial sites. Hexagrams contain both surface as well as veiled meanings that are not immediately obvious. In Yin feng shui, hexagrams reveal the correct way of orienting the gravesite. How trigrams evolved into hexagrams is illustrated in the circular expressions of yin and yang shown in the hexagram map on the following page.

THE 8 TRIGRAMS ARRANGED IN THE YIN ARRANGEMENT

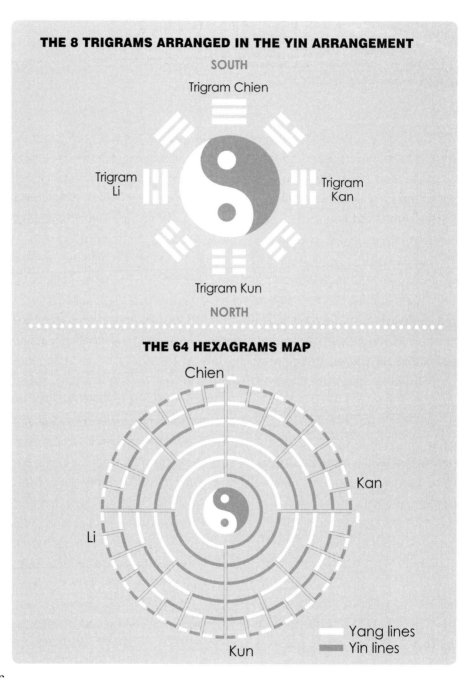

SOUTH

Trigram Chien

Trigram Li

Trigram Kan

Trigram Kun

NORTH

THE 64 HEXAGRAMS MAP

Chien

Kan

Li

Kun

Yang lines
Yin lines

26 MEANING OF THE TRIGRAMS

Each of the eight trigrams has different attributes and meanings, which are significant in understanding and interpreting the different feng shui charts of houses and buildings derived from compass formulas. Every trigram has a different symbolism; and their arrangement around the sides of the Pa Kua contains meanings for each of the directions which the sides represent.

Feng Shui practitioners of the Compass School make extensive references to the trigrams. This is because the meanings of the trigrams offer valuable "clues" on how to proceed with arranging space to maximize feng shui. Not only do trigrams correspond to compass directions, they are also rich with other connotations, attributes and meanings.

Each of the trigrams represents one of the five elements expressed either as a soft or dark aspect and they have a yin or yang dimension. So each trigram signifies a specific member of the family, an aspiration, an internal organ, a season, a musical note and other attributes. Knowing some of the more important of these attributes is what enables the practitioner to make important correlations for feng shui practice.

The meanings of the trigrams and their relationship to each other are significant in expanding the scope of feng shui practice. They tell us what can be "activated", and how their meanings can be interpreted in the physical realm to bring about auspicious outcomes. The eight trigrams are CHIEN the Creative, KUN the Receptive, CHEN the Arousing, SUN the Gentle, TUI the Joyous, KEN, keeping Still, KAN the Abysmal, and LI the Clinging.

THE EIGHT TRIGRAMS

Yang	Yin	Yin	Yang	Yin	Yang	Yang	Yin
Trigram Chien	Trigram Tui	Trigram Li	Trigram Chen	Trigram Sun	Trigram Kan	Trigram Ken	Trigram Kun

The table above shows the symbols and names of the 8 trigrams. Their yin or yang nature is also revealed.

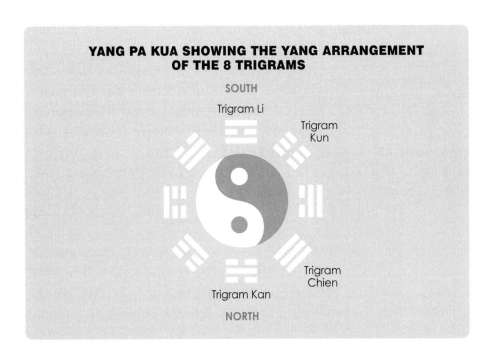

YANG PA KUA SHOWING THE YANG ARRANGEMENT OF THE 8 TRIGRAMS

SOUTH

Trigram Li

Trigram Kun

Trigram Chien

Trigram Kan

NORTH

27 | THE EIGHT TRIGRAMS

Chien

Kun

THE TRIGRAM "CHIEN", the Creative, comprises three unbroken lines. Its nature is YANG and it is associated with the FATHER, the head of the household, the patriarch, the male paternal. Chien also signifies HEAVEN, the sky, celestial spheres, strength, activity, power, brightness, bright colors, energy and perseverance. Chien doubled, forms the Hexagram of the I-Ching whose power is to be interpreted in a dual sense i.e. in terms of the strong creative action of the Deity of the Universe and in terms of the creative action of rulers or leaders in the world of Mankind. The element associated with Chien is big metal, and its symbolic animal is the HORSE, denoting power, endurance, firmness and strength. Additional symbols of the Creative include jade, which is itself the symbol of purity and firmness, round and circular objects, cold and ice. Its compass direction is South in the yin Arrangement of the Pa-Kua, and Northwest in the yang arrangement. In Yang feng shui, the direction of Chien is Northwest whose number is 6 and whose element is metal.

THE TRIGRAM "KUN", the Receptive is made up of three broken lines. The broken lines represent the dark, yielding, receptive, primal power of YIN. The attribute of this trigram refers to the MOTHER, the female maternal and devotion; and its image is the whole EARTH, which knows no partiality. The animal symbolizing Kun is the COW with a calf, symbolizing fertility. Kun is the perfect complement of Chien, the Creative (complement and not opposite because the Receptive does not combat the Creative but rather completes it). Kun signifies NATURE, in contrast to spirit, Earth in contrast to Heaven, Space against Time, the Female Maternal as against the Male Paternal.

In the interpretations of Kun in respect of the destiny of mankind, and when applied to human affairs, the relationship between Chien and Kun refers not only to the man-woman relationship but also to that of the prince and the minister, the father and the son, employer and employee, and so forth.

According to the I-Ching's commentary, Kun the Receptive must be activated and led by Chien the Creative if it is to maximize its benevolent essence. The compass direction of Kun is North in the yin arrangement, but in yang feng shui, it is Southwest. Its element is earth and its number is 2.

THE TRIGRAM "CHEN", the Arousing is made up of two broken Yin lines above an unbroken Yang Line. The trigram represents the eldest son and is often associated with movement and decision-making, vehemence and shock. Its image is thunder, and the dragon, rising out from the depths, soars magnificently up to the stormy skies, symbolizes it. A single strong line pushing upward below the two yielding lines represents this. This trigram is represented by dark yellow color, spreading outwards, which suggests the luxuriant growth of spring that covers the Earth with a garment of plants. The Element of this trigram is big wood.

In the I-Ching, the doubling of this trigram forms the Hexagram Chen, which is described as "shock, arousing fear, which in turn makes one cautious, and caution brings good fortune, a symbol of inner calm in the midst of the storm of outer movement". Chen also signifies thunder, "the kind which terrifies for miles around, a symbol of a mighty ruler who knows how to make himself respected yet is careful and exact in the smallest detail". Chen is placed Northeast in the yin arrangement and East in the yang sequence. In yang feng shui, we use East as the direction that signifies Chen. Its element is wood and its number is 3.

THE TRIGRAM "SUN", the Gentle, is formed by two unbroken yang lines above a broken yin line. This trigram represents the eldest daughter and its attribute is summed up in the word "penetrating". The gentle is small wood, it is the wind, it is indecision. The cockerel whose voice pierces the still morning air symbolizes it. Among men, it means those with broad foreheads, those with much white in their eyes; it means those close to making gains, so that in the market they get threefold value. Sun is sometimes interpreted as a sign of vehemence. Sun also represents white and whiteness, which is sometimes regarded as the color of the yin principle and sometimes as the yang. Here yin is in the lowest place at the beginning. Sun is placed Southwest in the yin arrangement and in Southeast in the yang arrangement. So in yang feng shui, we use Southeast to represent Sun. Its element is wood and its number is 4.

THE TRIGRAM "TUI", the Joyous, comprises one broken yin line above two unbroken yang lines. The two yang lines are considered the rulers of the trigram although they are incapable of acting as governing rulers. Tui represents joy, happiness and the youngest daughter. Tui is the element small metal. It is also the LAKE, which refreshes all living things.

Tui is the mouth; and this signifies to give joy to one another through one's feelings. A yin line becomes manifest above two yang lines; this show how the two principles give joy to each other and is manifested outwardly. Tui also means dropping off and bursting open. Among kinds of soil, it is hard and salty. It is the concubine, an association derived from the youngest daughter connections. It is the sheep, which is outwardly weak and inwardly stubborn, as suggested by the form of the Trigram. In the yin Arrangement, the trigram is placed Southeast, but in the yang arrangement it is placed WEST, so this is the direction which is used to signify Sun in the application of formulas for yang dwellings. Its element is metal and its number is 7.

THE TRIGRAM "KEN", Keeping Still, comprises an unbroken yang line above two broken yin lines. Ken represents the youngest son in the family. The trigram literally means standing still, a situation exemplified by the image of the mountain. This symbol of the mountain is of mysterious significance. Here, in the deep hidden stillness, the end of everything is joined to make a new beginning. Death and life, dying and resurrection – these are thoughts awakened by the transition from an old year to a new year. Ken thus signifies a time of solitude that is also the link between an ending and a beginning.

The element signified by Ken is small earth; and under the yin sequence of the trigrams, it is placed in the Northwest. Under the yang arrangement, Ken is Northeast. Its element is earth and its number is 8.

THE TRIGRAM "KAN", the Abysmal, is made up of one unbroken yang line sandwiched between two broken yin lines. Kan represents the MIDDLE SON. Its element is WATER, and its season is WINTER. Kan signifies craftiness and hidden things. It is considered as a sign of Danger and Melancholia because one (strong) yang line is hemmed in by two (weak) yin lines. The symbolic color of Kan is red, i.e. the red that resembles the fluid of the body i.e. blood. Kan was originally placed West in the yin arrangement, but was moved to the North under the yang arrangement, the place formerly occupied by Kun, the Receptive. Thus in yang dwelling feng shui Kan is signified by the direction North and its element is water so its colour is blue or black. The number of Kan is 1.

THE TRIGRAM "LI", the Clinging, is made up of one broken line in the center hemmed in by two strong yang lines. Li is FIRE, and represents the MIDDLE DAUGHTER. Li is also the sun, brightness, lightning, heat and dryness. The character of the trigram suggests something firm on the outside but hollow, weak and yielding within. This trigram strongly implies dependence, but the kind of dependence which is positive and nourishing, as when the plant "clings" to the soil and grows, or when "the sun and the moon attain their brightness by clinging to heaven". The yielding element in Li is the central line; hence its image is of a strong yet docile type of cow.

Fire flames upwards, hence the phrase, "that which is bright rises". In the spiritual sense, the brightness of this trigram offers the potential for its light to "illuminate" the world. Li occupies the East in the yin arrangement and its place under the yang arrangement is the South, which represents the summer sun illuminating all earthly things. So in applying the formulas for yang dwellings, feng shui uses South to be the direction of Li. Its number is 9 and its element is fire.

28 TWO ARRANGEMENTS OF TRIGRAMS

The 8 trigrams collectively symbolize a trinity of world principles recognized as the Subject (man), the Object having form (earth) and the Content (heaven). The bottom line is Earth; the middle is Man; and the top line is Heaven. A significant feature of the trigrams is that they transform, and in doing so they create new aspects. This is why we have two arrangements of the trigrams around the eight compass directions, referred to as the Early Heaven or yin arrangement and the Later Heaven or yang arrangement. These two arrangements are placed in two kinds of Pa Kuas – the Yin Pa Kua and Yang Pa Kua.

In the Early Heaven YIN Arrangement, the transformation is expressed as four pairs of trigrams described lyrically as follows:
- as "Heaven and Earth determining the directions" signified by Chien and Kun;
- as "Mountain and Lake uniting" (Tui and Ken);
- as "Thunder and Wind arousing each other" (Chen and Sun), and
- as "Water and Fire (Kan and Li) not combating" each other.

This summary of the trigram relationships reflect their arrangement in the Early Heaven or YIN Pa Kua. These descriptions feature in the application of Yin feng shui of gravesites. In the Later Heaven YANG Arrangement, the trigrams express a seasonal and cyclical relationship, so their locations in the Pa Kua change and the nature of this change has feng shui formula implications. Anyone wishing to master compass formula feng shui should develop strong familiarity with these two types of Pa Kuas where the 8 trigrams are placed differently around the compass.

YIN PA KUA
EARLY HEAVEN TRIGRAM ARRANGEMENT

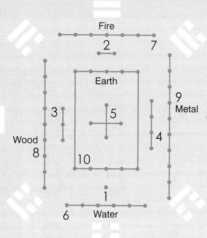

YANG PA KUA
LATER HEAVEN TRIGRAM ARRANGEMENT

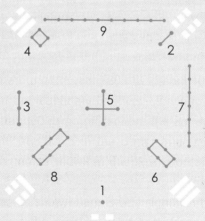

29 THE YIN PA KUA

The Yin arrangement of the trigrams gives rise to the YIN PA KUA. In this arrangement, the eight trigrams are named in a sequence of pairs. This Early Sequence formation is known as the Primal Arrangement. The original founder Fu Hsi discovered this sequence, and under this arrangement, the two important trigrams, Chien and Kun, which are the Creative and the Receptive, Heaven and Earth, are in the South and North compass points respectively. Chien is totally Yang and Kun is totally Yin and in the early heaven arrangement, they manifest as the North-South axis.

Then follows the Ken and Tui axis, i.e. the Mountain and the Lake; their forces are inter-related, in that the wind blows from the mountain to the lake while clouds and mist rise from the lake to the mountain. The relationship suggested is thus circular. The Ken-Tui axis is represented by the directions Northwest and Southeast in this Yin arrangement. The third axis is formed by Chen and Sun, i.e. Thunder and Wind, which strengthen each other whenever they emerge. This is positioned Northeast and Southwest.

Finally, the trigrams Li and Kan, which are Fire and Water, make up the concluding axis. Though these two elements appear at first to be irreconcilable opposites in the physical world, according to Fu Hsi, in their primal or "original" state, they balance each other so there is in reality no conflict between them at all. It is vital to understand this special relationship between the two most destructive and also most powerful elements. While they appear to be clashing, these two elements have the potential to harness great power.

In this Early Heaven sequence, fire and water occupy East and West respectively and their equivalent numbers here 3 and 7 placed East and West add up to the most auspicious 10. So the early heaven relationship between these two elements suggests some powerful force within. Note the sum of 10 prevails in ALL the four pairs of trigrams, suggesting an inner strength to the combinations.

It is suggested that when the trigrams move and intermingle, a double movement is observed: first, the usual clockwise movement, which is cumulative and expanding, so this forward movement determines events which come to pass; second, there is also an opposite backward motion, which folds and contracts, even as time passes, thereby creating "seeds" for the future. The explanation is that if the essence of this backward movement is understood, then the situation of the future unfolds clearly. This is the basis for the Yin Pa Kua arrangement being so excellent for deciphering yin feng shui and for the placement and orientation of tombs to ensure success for descendants.

The Primal Arrangement expresses the forces of nature in terms of "pairs of opposite". Thus Thunder, an electrically charged force, has Wind as its opposite. Rain, which moistens the seeds and enables them to germinate has the Sun, which supplies warmth, as its opposite. This example demonstrates the contention that "water and fire do not combat each other". In comprehending opposite moving forces, consider the trigram Ken, keeping still whose situation describes termination of expansion and growth. Its "opposite", the Joyous, brings forth "the harvest". Consider also the forces of the Creative and the Receptive, which represent the great laws of existence; these two comprise a pairing of opposites.

These explanations suggest ascending and descending forces which reveal the "secrets of the future". The Primal Arrangement expresses Heaven's view of existence. Such understanding however was frequently beyond the modest faculties of most people.

30   THE YANG PA KUA

This is the Later Heaven Arrangement of the trigrams and is also known as the "Inner World" Arrangement. In this arrangement, the trigrams are taken out of their groupings in pairs of opposites and are placed instead in a circular temporal progression of their manifestations in the physical earth realm. Under this yang arrangement, the cardinal points and seasons are related. There is a clear perception of cycles and seasonal, monthly and daily influences.

The arrangement of the trigrams around the Pa Kua is thus drastically altered.

The description of the Later Heaven Arrangement of the trigrams in the Yang Pa Kua shows the creative activity of God in the trigram CHEN, the Arousing, which stands in the East and signifies Spring (the beginning).

All living things come forth in the sign of the Arousing. They come to completion in the sign of the gentle (SUN) which stands in the Southeast. Completion means that all creatures become pure and perfect. The Clinging (LI) is the brightness in which all creatures perceive one another. It is the trigram of the South.

Thus the sages turn to the South (i.e. to the light) whenever they give ear to the meaning of the Universe. Next comes KUN, the Receptive, which means the Earth. The Earth ensures that all creatures are nourished. TUI or Joyous comes in mid autumn, followed by CHIEN the Creative in the Northwest, and KAN the Water in the North.

Here in this sign of the Abysmal all creatures work. This is followed by the sign of the KEN, Keeping Still like the mountain, in the Northeast, where the beginning and the end find completion. Thus the cycle ends.

The sequence of the trigrams reflects the harmony and balance in the year. What is narrated in the above description is the cycle of seasons and the cycle of nature. Trigrams are allotted to the seasons and to points of the compass to reflect the harmony of nature.

One can extend the annual cycle to that of an ordinary day, so for instance the Trigram CHEN while signifying Spring is also representative of morning, the start of the day. The next trigram SUN represents the wind, which melts the ice of winter, and wood, which germinates and grows. This takes us to LI, midsummer or noon time (of the day), with the remaining trigrams showing the way round the cycle, all the while stressing harmony and balance.

The Later Heaven Arrangement of the Yang Pa Kua is more easily understood. It is also more applicable to yang houses as its basic premise reflects life in the Earth realm. In view of this, all latter day practices of Chinese feng shui use this sequential representation of the Pa Kua to unlock the meanings of the Luo Pan's compass directions when analyzing the chi energy of yang dwellings.

The Chinese calendar system of Heavenly Stems and Earthly Branches relate to the Later Heaven Arrangement of the Pa-Kua, as do many of Compass Feng Shui's formulas. For this reason, all feng shui Luo Pans contain this arrangement of the trigrams in one of its inner rings.

31 THE EFFECT OF ROADS

The arrangements of the trigrams around the two Pa Kuas – Yin and Yang – reveal the effect of surrounding rivers on one's home or office building with amazing accuracy. This movement of the trigrams from its location in the Yin Pa Kua to its place in the Yang Pa Kua reveals how surrounding rivers can affect the luck of houses. This depends on how they move towards the house/building from one direction and exit in another direction.

The same interpretation can also be analyzed for roads that are in the vicinity of your home. Generally, when water or roads flow towards the home from a Yin Pa Kua direction and flows out in a Yang Pa Kua direction, the water or road reflects luck coming from heaven and flowing to earth and is thus auspicious for yang houses. Moving in the other direction is not auspicious and suggests illness, death or loss.

Take note of the summary of the Yin Pa Kua and Yang Pa Kua of directions based on the trigram placements in the two Pa Kuas, then note that when roads or rivers near your home flow in the following way, they are said to be auspicious for the home.

Thus: The trigram CHIEN moves from South to the Northwest, so when roads or rivers come towards the home from the South and moves away in a Northwesterly direction, the road is auspicious and benefits the father of the household.

The trigram KUN moves from North to the Southwest, so when roads or rivers move towards the home from the North and move away in a Southwesterly direction, the road is auspicious and benefits the mother in the household.

The trigram LI moves from East to South, so when roads or rivers move towards the home from the East and move away in a South direction, the road is auspicious and benefits the middle daughter in the household.

The trigram KAN moves from West to North, so when roads or rivers move towards the home from the West and move away in a Northerly direction, the road is auspicious and benefits the middle son in the household.

The trigram TUI moves from Southeast to West, so roads or rivers moving towards the home from the Southeast and moving away in a Westerly direction are auspicious and benefit the youngest daughter in the household.

The trigram KEN moves from Northwest to Northeast, so roads or rivers moving towards the home from the Northwest and moving away in a Northeasterly direction are auspicious and benefit the youngest son in the household.

The trigram CHEN moves from Northeast to East, so roads or rivers moving towards the home from the Northeast and moving away in an Easterly direction are auspicious and benefit the eldest son in the household.

The trigram SUN moves from Southwest to Southeast, so roads or rivers moving towards the home from the Southwest and moving away in a Southeasterly direction are auspicious and benefit the eldest daughter in the household.

32 THE FIVE ELEMENTS

The theory of the five elements is an important foundation of formula feng shui. In Chinese, this is known as "Wu Xing", translated as "five elements", although it actually means much more. The word "Wu" means "five" and "Xing" is a way of saying " five types of chi dominating at different times". This has been shortened to the word "elements" which has become conventionally accepted in the language of feng shui. The five elements are water, wood, fire, earth and metal.

Water dominates in winter, wood in spring, fire in summer, and metal in autumn. At the intersection between two seasons, the transitional period is dominated by earth. The names "water", "wood", "fire", "metal" and "earth" refer to substances whose properties resemble the respective element and help us understand the different properties of the five types of chi.

The properties of the five types of chi are summarized as follows:

WATER: Water runs downwards. Water signifies wealth and success related with money, but there is always the danger of overflow. The element of water can bring enormous wealth luck or it can cause great loss. Water is a powerful element that cuts both ways. One cannot have too much or too little of water. In the compass formulas, water is extremely important and special attention must be given to water if what you want is to gain extra income or improve your monetary lifestyle with feng shui. Water thus is always symbolic of a money flow. Whether the money flows inwards or outwards is the key to getting it right!

WOOD: Wood grows upwards and outwards like a tree, so wood always suggests growth and expansion. Think of a seed growing into a tall and luxuriant tree filled with blossoms and flowers. The chi of wood pushes upwards. If success and expansion is what you need and want, look at the best ways to activate the wood element. For this reason, a luxuriant growth of plants in the East and Southeast is always beneficial, and indicates very good feng shui.

FIRE: Fire spreads in all directions. It is radiant and hot, and needs to be controlled. Fire has the potential to suddenly become so big that it can get out of control. Fire brings fame, recognition and luminosity, the kind of success that but it is can also burn itself out. Think of it brightening the sky with its flashing red and yellow, but also make sure the fire is controlled. Fire energy leaps in all directions. Fire, like water, is powerful, but like water it is a double edged sword. It can be so hot as to burn chi to ashes. Fire is for success, recognition and popularity.

METAL: Metal pierces inwards, and is sharp and pointed. It can be deadly and powerful, but it is also the easiest element to control. This is because as an element it is deemed to be unbending and true to type. Metal does not surprise anyone. It is a cold type of chi which when properly harnessed brings enormous power. Metal chi stands for power and authority. The danger of metal is its unbending nature. Metal when energized can be relentless in its strength. Always have fire energy ready and nearby to ensure that metal is always under control.

EARTH: The chi of the earth is warm and embracing. It nurtures and nourishes. Earth energy is protective. It takes care of the home when it is properly energized. Of the five elements, earth is the friendliest and also the most important to have. The Earth element must be steady and strong, then the essence of good fortune is present.

| WATER | WOOD | FIRE | EARTH | METAL |

Earth is also representative of the center of any home, so do keep note of the importance of this element. At the same time one must also realize that Earth can turn dangerous, as when it appears as a result of flying star numbers that bring illness, loss and accidents. This represents the darker side of the earth element.

In Flying Star feng shui, the two most afflicted numbers - i.e. 5 and 2 - belong to the Earth element. These bring misfortune and illness, thus must be suppressed with metal energy. But the auspicious number 8 also belongs to the Earth element. As we are currently in the period of 8, we are said to be in an Earth period.

ATTRIBUTES OF
THE FIVE ELEMENTS

n terms of attributes, the five elements are associated with seasons, directions, numbers and so forth. The table below given a summary of the different attributes indicated by each element.

	WOOD	WATER	FIRE	METAL	EARTH
Season	Spring	Winter	Summer	Autumn	Between
Direction	East/SE	North	South	West/NW	SW/NE
Color	Green	Black/Blue	Red	White	Ochre/Brown
Shape	Rectangle	Wavy	Triangular	Round	Square
Energy	Outwards	Descending	Upwards	Inwards	Sideways
Numbers	3, 4	1	9	6, 7	2, 5, 8
Body Organ	Liver	Kidney	Eyes	Lungs	Stomach/womb
Taste	Sour	Salty	Bitter	Pungent	Sweet

Each element has its own shape attribute, colors, type of energy and numbers. Each also symbolizes different inner organs and outer parts of the body. The list given here is far from complete as there are many more connotations associated with the elements, but these are the most common attributes.

The five elements hold the key to unlocking the meanings of the different formulas of feng shui. In addition to the elements allotted to each of the eight cardinal and primary directions, each of the 24 mountain directions also has a different set of elements. All the elements assigned to the directions are then used to analyze the different meanings and quality of chi under different methods of feng shui.

The five elements also play a significant role in interpreting destiny charts, and features strongly in the diagnosis of disease and ailments in traditional Chinese medicine.

In Eight Mansions and Flying Star feng shui, understanding the cycles and interactions of the elements adds a fantastic dimension in the interpreting of house charts. The elements and their cycles also provide excellent clues on how to cure, remedy, activate and energize the different sectors of the house or office.

34 THREE CYCLES OF INTERACTIONS

Feng shui analysis requires total familiarity with the five elements. But even more important than their different attributes is to know about the three cycles of relationships between the elements. The three cycles of relationships or interactions are the productive cycle, the destructive cycle and the exhaustive cycle.

Actually there are two primary cycles of interaction that govern the relationship of the elements, and these are cycles of either production or destruction. When any two elements are in a productive cycle, they give rise to harmony, and when they are in a destructive cycle, they give rise to disharmony.

The **productive cycle** is where wood produces fire, fire produces earth, earth produces metal, metal produces water and water produces wood with the cycle starting all over again.

The **destructive cycle** is when water destroys fire, fire destroys metal, metal destroys wood, wood destroys earth, earth destroys water and the cycle starts again.

There is a third cycle and this is the **exhaustive cycle**. In this cycle, the productive cycle reverts backwards. Thus fire exhausts wood, earth exhausts fire, metal exhausts earth, water exhaust metal, wood exhausts water and the cycle starts again.

It is this third cycle of the five elements that is so useful for designing powerful cures and remedies that can overcome afflictions caused by the intangible forces of bad flying stars or afflicted directions. The cycles of the five element relationships are illustrated in the graphic below.

For simple application of element enhancement, commit to memory the element categorization of shapes, seasons, numbers, directions, objects and so forth. Then at the most elementary level of the practice, systematically identify the elements in each corner of your home, and move them around to achieve harmony by making sure no conflict of elements occur in any corner of your home. Instead, try introducing symbolic and element enhancers that strengthen the chi of every corner. This is symbolic feng shui using the compass.

THE CYCLES OF FIVE ELEMENTS

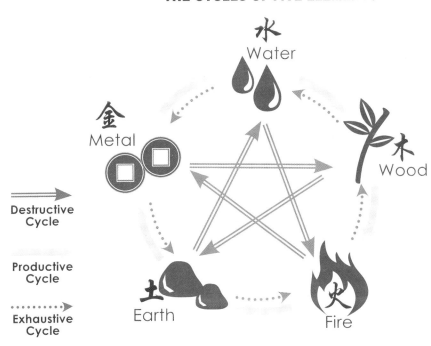

35 FENG SHUI BASED ON ELEMENTS

The five elements of each of the eight directions give rise to basic feng shui guidelines, and these offer suggestions on how the feng shui of different sectors can be enhanced. Here are four basic guidelines to commit to memory.

1. Refrain from having too much water in the SOUTH because water destroys the fire element of the South! But when the flying stars indicate it is auspicious to place water here, you can do so, because the water will then be energizing special water energy here. Nevertheless, the water feature should never be so big as to overwhelm and conquer the fire completely. Otherwise wealth will be attained at the price of your good name.

2. Try not to place round extensions, semi-circular windows or anything circular in the EAST or SOUTHEAST part of your home. This is because round is the shape that symbolizes metal and metal destroys the wood element of the East. Instead, the East is best activated with the presence of water. A water lily pond filled with live guppies is an excellent way to bring out the best of the chi of this corner. This is because water produces wood and is thus good for the East.

3. In the NORTH it is excellent to have round and circular structures, since the element of this shape is entirely harmonious with this corner of the home. Round is metal which produces water. What is bad however are earth element objects like stones, pebbles and boulders. It is definitely not a good idea to build a Zen garden made predominantly of stone in the North part of the home.

4. In the WEST or NORTHWEST, which are metal corners, placing earth element objects is extremely auspicious. Thus stone sculptures, stone pathways, crystal decorative trees and raw natural crystal geodes are very auspicious here. What should not be in these corners are fire element objects such as bright lights and excessive amounts of red.

5. In the SOUTHWEST and NORTHEAST, the best objects to activate and strengthen the chi here are objects that belong to the fire element. So anything red is gloriously auspicious. Bright chandelier lights are also excellent, as are crystals.

Crystal money tree, ideal for activating wealth luck in the West and Northwest.

THE LO SHU SQUARE

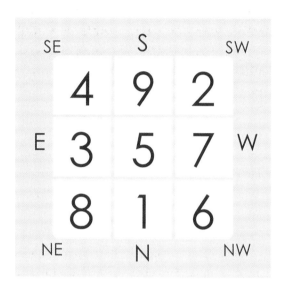

I n attempting to unlock the secrets of the compass, ancient and latter day scholars have focused attention on the mysterious Lo Shu magic square of nine numbers.

It is believed that at or around the year 2205 BC (about 4000 years ago), a noble Tortoise emerged from the legendary Lo River, carrying on its huge back nine numbers that were arranged in a grid pattern. The Lo Shu square of numbers was arranged with the number 5 in the center and the rest of the numbers distributed around the grid as shown in the illustration above.

The pattern of numbers as shown here is very significant to learning feng shui correctly. It is what gives the greatest potency to feng shui's many formulas.

This is because this Lo Shu arrangement of numbers contains the secret key to unlocking countless ways of using directions to manipulate the chi of the environment. This is done through the interpretation of flying star natal charts.

The numbers of the Lo Shu are arranged in such a way that adding them in whatever direction along any three points in a straight line (whether horizontally, vertically or diagonally) add up to the same number i.e. 15. This coincides with the number of days it takes for a waxing or waning cycle of the moon.

The Lo Shu sequence of numbers is crucial to unlocking the auspicious and inauspicious days of the almanac. It is also the Lo Shu numbers of the Chinese Hsia calendar which enables those who know how to calculate good and bad days for undertaking a variety of life rituals - getting married, celebrating birthdays, launching projects and so forth.

Feng shui masters also came to realize that the Lo Shu numbers held the secrets to understanding time feng shui as it applied to space. Thus the Lo Shu numbers and their sequence of movement around the grids of the square became the basis of formulating the flying star natal chart.

In fact, the flying star natal chart is expressed exactly the same way that the Lo Shu chart is expressed (see diagram here). How the numbers are placed as stars into natal charts makes up the formula of Flying Star feng shui.

All the most crucial aspects of this formula is condensed into the flying star rings of the Luo Pan. Knowing how to use Flying Star enables anyone to unlock all the most potent secrets of the Luo Pan. The pattern of numbers of the Lo Shu is connected with the trigrams of the Later Heaven Pa Kua. We shall be meeting the many permutations and transformations of the Lo Shu numbers throughout the course of this book.

37   THE HO TU SQUARE

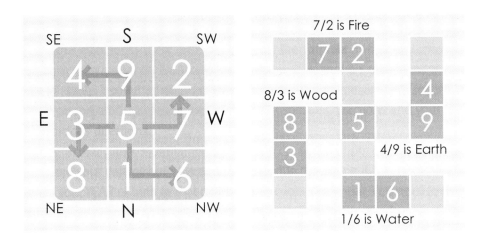

The Lo Shu was by no means the first pattern of numbers. 900 years earlier, around 2943 BC, Chinese myths claim that Fu Hsi had received a formation of numbers, which, according to legend, was brought to him on the back of a Dragon Horse that emerged out of the Yellow River!

This particular pattern of numbers, referred to as the Ho Tu Pattern of numbers (shown here) was arranged in four pairs of odd and even numbers with 5 in the center. The significance of the Ho Tu combination lie in the way the numbers are combined, 1 with 6; 2 with 7, 3 with 8, and 4 with 9. Notice that these combinations are pairs of yin and yang, odd and even, male and female numbers. All odd numbers are yang and male, while all even numbers are yin and female.

The Ho Tu combinations define auspicious circumstances when they occur. Thus later on when you see them as combinations in the flying star natal charts, learn to recognize them because they indicate good fortune. How to find out if your house has any of these combinations of numbers is revealed when you study Flying Star feng shui. Also when you start to compute your KUA numbers under Eight Mansions, take note that couples who have KUA numbers that reflect the Ho Tu combinations are likely to have very happy marriages.

The combination of 1 and 6 signifies wealth as this is placed North which is water. The number 1 prevails here, as it is a yang number. The number 6 is metal which produces water. When this combination is present in your flying star chart, activate it with a water feature such as a water lily bowl or a fish pond.

The combination of 3 and 8 signifies wood as this is placed East. Here the number 3 prevails as it is wood. Combined with earth, wood prevails. In period 8, this combination is most auspicious as it means growth and expansion. Activate this combination with a healthy lush plant if you have it in your flying star chart.

The combination of 2 and 7 signifies fire and is placed South. Here the elements combined are earth and metal, thereby creating earth. This combination is extremely brilliant when it is near a mountain, so if you see it in your flying star chart, create a mountain with stones and crystals in the part of the home that has this combination. This combination brings relationship and charisma luck.

The combination 4 and 9 signifies metal or gold. It is placed in the West. Here the combination is of wood and fire, which produces the element of fire. But the element here is gold. So here we see a situation that indicates a pairing between two people who become famous and powerful. If this combination appears in your flying star chart, activate with lots of activity and you will enjoy extremely powerful success luck.

The mystical attributes of the Lo Shu Grid have occupied religious and philosophical scholars through the ages and survives today as an acknowledged mystery, still potent, and still guarding its secrets. In reality however, the Ho Tu is more mysterious and one reason it is not more famous is because Ho Tu numbers are applied more in YIN feng shui and rarely in YANG feng shui, except as advanced interpretations of flying star charts.

THE HO TU COMBINATIONS AND THEIR MEANINGS

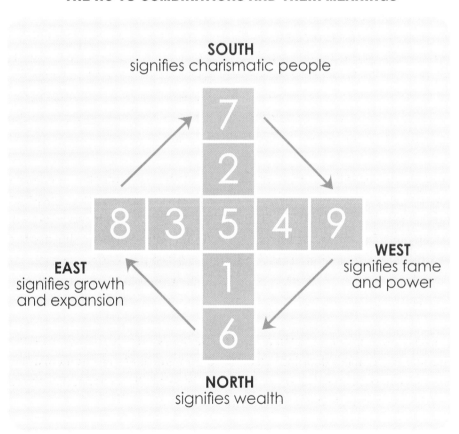

SOUTH
signifies charismatic people

EAST
signifies growth
and expansion

WEST
signifies fame
and power

NORTH
signifies wealth

38 THE THREE PLATES OF THE COMPASS

Compass formula feng shui differentiates between the three plates of the compass, which are the Heaven Plate, the Earth Plate and the Mankind Plate.

The HEAVEN PLATE

This plate moves faster than the EARTH Plate and is usually 7.5 degrees ahead of the EARTH Plate (to the left). The measurement of North in this plate is described as the True North and is based on the sundial. The HEAVEN plate is used to check the quality of water flows and whether they are auspicious or inauspicious. Here we are referring to the inflow and outflow of water. So the Heaven plate is sometimes referred to as the Water Plate.

However, the HEAVEN Plate is also used for doing the feng shui (and water flows) of YIN houses i.e. the burial plots of ancestors in cemeteries. It is believed that Yin feng shui and Yin water are very powerful in determining the fortunes of descendants. This potency is legendary and till today there are feng shui masters who proffer yin feng shui advice. This branch of feng shui is not suitable for mass dissemination. However, it is useful to know that the traditional Heaven plate Luo Pan contains many secrets of Yin feng shui.

It is also used to provide alternatives for emptiness and death lines, so if the direction of the main door indicated falls on an emptiness line, some masters use the Heaven Plate solution by adding 7.5 degrees to the door direction to see if under the new plate the direction turns auspicious.

THE MANKIND PLATE

This plate is slower than the EARTH PLATE and is thus 7.5 degrees behind the EARTH PLATE (towards the right). This difference is due to the different NORTH. In the MANKIND plate, the North is measured according to the position of the Polaris Star, and thus translates each of the 24 mountains into elements according to the stars of the constellation.

This plate is used to determine the feng shui of surrounding rocks, hills, mountains, tall buildings and rivers, and their location vis a vis the house is to be checked. The formula for this uses the five elements, so that the element of the house and that of surrounding structures are contained in the 24 mountains chart based on the MANKIND plate. The element relationship between the two determines if surrounding mountains and elevations will bring "gold" for the home, or whether they will bring afflictions. This formula makes it possible to determine whether surrounding buildings and structures are good for any house.

THE EARTH PLATE

In the Earth plate, NORTH refers to the Magnetic North. Most Luo Pans that deal with the feng shui of YANG houses are based on the EARTH plate and this is the plate that is of most direct relevance to most feng shui practitioners.

The EARTH Plate is also known as the Middle Plate. The directions and elements of the 24 mountains that are used to apply Eight Mansions as well as Flying Star feng shui are based on the EARTH Plate. All formulas using this plate use Magnetic North to derive their compass measurements. So using an ordinary western-style compass is acceptable. For this same reason, those living in the Southern hemisphere can be assured that everything in this book applies in exactly the same way in both hemispheres.

THE EARTH PLATE

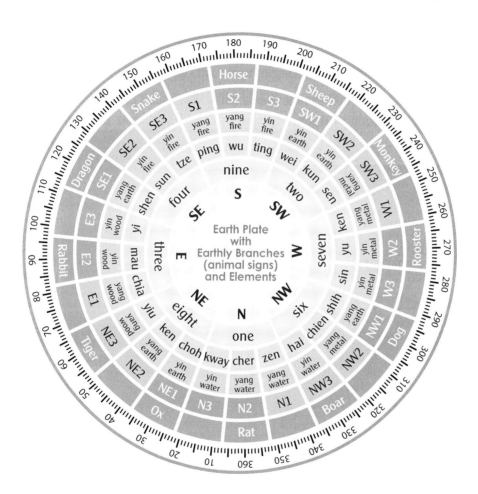

There are usually 24 directions marked out in the Earth Plate (also known as the Middle Plate) which is the compass used in Flying Star feng shui. This plate contains the 24 directions most frequently used in compass-based feng shui for yang type dwellings. The EARTH PLATE unlocks many beneficial secrets of compass feng shui.

Flying Star teaches the practitioner to cast the feng shui chart of any building using the facing direction of the building. The formula shows how the numbers are filled into the different grids of the chart and also how they move around the chart whether in a yin or yang mode. This is based on the yin and yang aspects of the 24 mountains of the Earth Plate. This determines how numbers are placed into the nine grids of a flying star chart.

The chart then reveals the nature and distribution of chi within buildings and homes. It is invaluable for identifying auspicious and inauspicious sectors of any building, and also for offering clues on how to enhance good fortune and protect against misfortune before it happens. This is the great wonder of Flying Star feng shui – when you know how to use it, you will be amazed by what it can do for you and your family in all aspects of your life.

The North direction of the EARTH PLATE is magnetic North. So a western style compass, which uses magnetic North, can be used when applying Flying Star. Those who have your own Luo Pan can use it to determine the directions, but any good western style compass, which enables you to identify the three subsectors of each of the eight directions, is also fine. Familiarize yourself with the 24 directions of the Earth plate. Study their elements and their yin/yang aspects. Note that the elements of these 24 directions are not the same under the different plates. In the beginning, the three plates can be confusing, but in Flying Star and Eight Mansions, you need only the EARTH PLATE directions.

40 THE MAN PLATE

The 24 mountains of the Man Plate are known as the Middle Ring 24 mountains. It lies 7.5 degrees to the right of the Earth Plate and this is because it is said that the Man Plate moves slower than the Earth Plate. Also the NORTH in this plate is not Magnetic North. Instead, it is Polaris North, and since the star Polaris is part of the constellation, the elements of the 24 mountains in this Plate reflect the stars and constellations. The elements of its 24 mountains are different from those in the Earth Plate.

In feng shui, the Man Plate is excellent for determining the impact of surrounding rock formations. In the old days, this compass was used to determine the auspiciousness or hostility of nearby mountains and valleys. In modern day environments however, feng shui masters have very effectively used this same formula to analyze the impact of buildings, towers, transmission lines and other city-type structures that surround any building.

Analysis is based entirely on the interaction of elements assigned to the house and to buildings in the vicinity of the house. In terms of practical usage therefore, this formula is excellent for checking how new buildings erected near you will affect the feng shui of your home. This investigation can be undertaken at two levels. You can investigate the effect on the whole house or you can investigate the impact on individual residents.

41 ASSESSING IMPACT OF BUILDINGS

To determine whether nearby buildings are beneficial, you need to determine the following:

1. the sitting direction of the house. This determines its element.
2. the KUA number of the resident
3. the direction of the nearby building whose feng shui effect we wish to analyze.

Determine the element of the house based on its sitting direction, and the element of nearby buildings using the Man Plate. An easy way to determine the directions using an ordinary compass is to measure the direction with an ordinary compass then deduct 7.5 degrees from the reading. This determines the sitting direction of the house and the direction of the building being investigated.

When the building is in a direction whose element produces the element of the house, the building will bring patronage and resource luck to residents.

When the building is in a direction whose element is similar to the element of the house, the building will bring prosperity to the residents.

When the building is in a direction whose element is destroyed by the element of the house, the building will cause residents to have money and servants.

When the building is in a direction whose element is produced by the element of the house, the building will exhaust/deplete the energy of the residents of the house.

When the building is in a direction whose element destroys the element of the house, the building will cause grave misfortune to befall the residents.

A good way to understand this formula is to look at a worked example.

Example: Let us investigate the effect of three BUILDINGS on a house that faces West 3 and so is sitting East 3. This makes its sitting element EARTH. What is the effect of the three buildings marked A, B and C on the fortunes of the house?

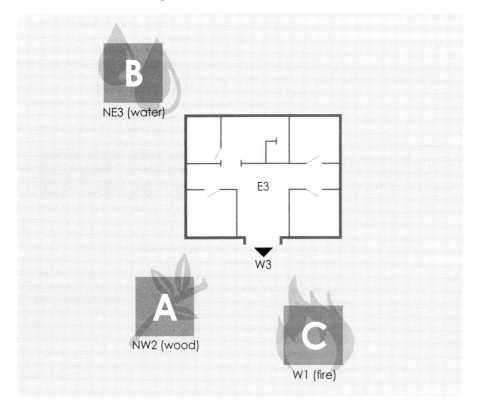

Firstly, Building A is in front of the house on its right and is located in the NW2 direction. The element of that direction is wood. Since wood destroys Earth, Building A will cause misfortune to befall the house. It is therefore necessary to counter the killing chi coming from that building.

The best thing to do is to hang a metal windchime in the NW2 direction as this will intercept the destructive chi coming from that direction. (Note that metal destroys wood). We can also hang red curtains in the NW2 direction, or install a bright light here to simulate fire energy. This will exhaust the killing chi emanating from the building.

Secondly, Building B, which is behind the house, is in the direction of NE3 and from the chart we can see this direction belongs to the water element. Since Earth destroys Water, this building is good for the house as it brings servants and money luck to the home. There is no need to enhance or do anything to this direction.

Thirdly, Building C is in West 1 direction, which is of the fire element. Since Fire produces Earth, this building creates excellent prosperity luck for the house. So a clear view of this building would be most beneficial. Indeed if you have a bright hall i.e. a small patch of empty space in the West 1 direction of your home, this should act as a magnet for the chi created by the building to flow benevolently towards you.

42 EFFECT OF BUILDINGS ON RESIDENTS

I t is also possible to investigate the effect of surrounding buildings on the luck of individual residents by using the KUA element of the resident for the analysis. This means that while nearby buildings affect the house in general, they also have effects on the individual residents of the household.

For those with KUA numbers 2, 5 or 8, the effect of the buildings will be exactly as analyzed for the house since the element of these numbers is Earth.

Those with KUA 1 – water will benefit from Buildings B and C, but Building A will be exhausting.

Those with KUA 9 – fire will benefit from Building A and C. But Building B will cause serious bad luck. To overcome, plant trees in that direction.

Those with KUA 3 and 4 – wood will benefit from Building A and B but not Building C.

Those with KUA 6 and 7 – metal will benefit from Building A, but will be Buildings B and C.

As an exercise, see if you can work out how we arrived at the above conclusions. As an aid in the analysis, you might want to refresh your knowledge of the three cycles of the five elements. Knowing how the five elements interact with each other is the key to this method.

43   THE HEAVEN PLATE

The 24 mountains of the Heaven Plate is usually found in the Sarn He Luo Pan (Three Harmony Luo Pan) and is used for investigating incoming and outgoing water flows for Yin dwellings.

In the old days, the feng shui of grave sites was deemed to be exceedingly important since it was believed that good water flows in the grave sites of one's ancestors had a direct bearing on the wealth of descendants. In modern times, Yin feng shui continues to be practiced, especially by wealthy families keen to ensure that their family wealth continues to stay intact and even expand. As I prefer to pass on this dimension of feng shui, Yin feng shui does not fall within the scope of this book. However, it is beneficial to know the context within which yin feng shui is practiced.

The Heaven Plate moves 7.5 degrees faster than the Earth Plate and uses True North, which is based on the Sun Dial, as the reference point of its compass directions. There are portions of the Three Harmony School on water flows that apply to both Yin and Yang dwellings. Yang dwellings are referred in the texts as 'dragons dens'. This refers to the water flow principles that must be followed based on the facing directions of houses and buildings.

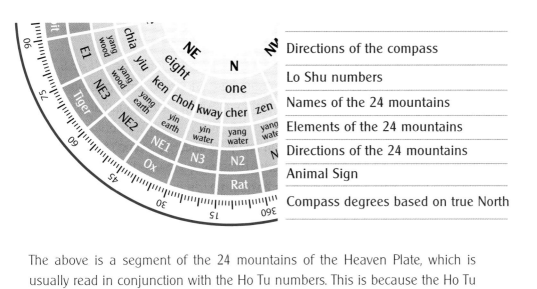

Directions of the compass

Lo Shu numbers

Names of the 24 mountains

Elements of the 24 mountains

Directions of the 24 mountains

Animal Sign

Compass degrees based on true North

The above is a segment of the 24 mountains of the Heaven Plate, which is usually read in conjunction with the Ho Tu numbers. This is because the Ho Tu numbers feature strongly in the Yin water formulas. This practice when applied to Yin dwellings is an advanced formula quite beyond the scope of the amateur practitioner, and in my opinion is a little impractical in the context of modern day restrictions on what one can do in graveyards.

44

EIGHT MANSION KUA FORMULA

I introduced this formula on personalized auspicious and inauspicious directions based on one's KUA number in my first international book on feng shui, the *Complete Illustrated Guide to Feng Shui* and I believe it was the sheer potency of this simple yet powerful formula that contributed to millions of people around the world getting interested in feng shui. The KUA formula works so amazingly it leaves us wanting to know more. The Kua formula got me hooked on feng shui, and I am certain it is the Kua formula that has opened many people's hearts and minds to the ancient practice of feng shui. Today, many people who know this formula (also known as Eight Mansions) practice it in some way or other. What is less known is that when used in tandem with the Flying Star formula, the KUA formula becomes even more potent in its effectiveness.

The KUA formula is based on one's date of birth and one's gender, and using these two pieces of information, all you have to do is work out what your KUA number is. Actually, it is the year of birth which is required. but because we need to find the lunar year equivalent of the birth year, starting with the date of birth is more efficient way of getting the correct Kua number.

Using your KUA number you can determine if you are a West or East group person; you will also know self element, your self trigram and lucky number – these personalized attributes enable you to personalize your feng shui customize the clothes you wear and the decorations and symbols you surround yourself with in order to attract good luck.

Eight Mansions or KUA formula feng shui is very simple, much easier than Flying Star; but when used together, the two formulas work incredibly fast. The KUA formula is a personalized formula so it applies to the feng shui of individuals, and not to the entire space. Flying Star however brings good feng shui to the entire household, so the two methods complement one another.

45 DETERMINING YOUR KUA NUMBER

The Eight Mansions formula involves calculating one's KUA number. KUA refers to one side of the Pa Kua, the eight sided symbol that shows the eight directions. There are two parts to the formula – first you need to calculate your personal KUA number and this is based on your gender and date of birth. From that number you determine if you are an EAST or WEST group person, and this determines your four auspicious directions and your four inauspicious directions.

You need your date of birth because you need to determine if it is necessary to adjust your YEAR of birth to that of the Chinese lunar calendar. You need to refer to the lunar calendar to see if your date of birth falls in the previous year. The lunar new year starts on a different western date each year sometime in January or February. So you require the lunar calendar to see if your year of birth needs adjustment.

Note that some masters use the solar calendar where the New Year date is deemed to be 4th February to make the adjustment to the Chinese calendar. I prefer to use the Chinese lunar calendar for greater accuracy. If you use the lunar calendar, do take note that this then differs from the calendar that is used for Flying Star calculations, which uses the solar, or HSIA, calendar. There is no need to feel confused by the two calendars. Just note that these two calendars are part of the Chinese system of measuring time.

To calculate your KUA number, take the last two digits of your year of birth and add the numbers. Keep adding them until you reduce them to a single digit.

If you are male, deduct this digit from 10 and the result is your KUA number. Note that for all male children born after 2000, you deduct from 9 to obtain the KUA number.

If you are female, add the digit to 5 and the result is your KUA number. If the result of adding 5 has two digits, keep adding until you get a single digit. Note that for all female children born after 2000, you add 6 instead of 5 to obtain the KUA number.

Example: Male born 7th June 1954: Since this man was born in June, there is no need to adjust for the lunar year and the year is taken to be 1954. The last two digits of year of birth is 5+4=9. And then 10-9=1 so the KUA number is 1.

Example: Female born 8th October 1975: Since this woman was born in October, there is no need to adjust for the lunar year and the year is taken to be 1975. The last two digits of year of birth is 7+5=12 so 1+2=3. And then 3+5=8 so the KUA number is 8.

From your KUA number you then derive your personal element and personal trigram. Your KUA number can also be regarded as your personal number. The table below gives you the elements and trigrams associated with the numbers 1 to 9.

KUA #	1	2	3	4	5	6	7	8	9
TRIGRAM	Kan	Kun	Chen	Sun	*	Chien	Tui	Ken	Li
ELEMENT	Water	Earth	Wood	Wood	*	Metal	Metal	Earth	Fire

*note: Males with KUA 5 changes it to 2, while females with KUA 5 changes it to 8

46 EAST OR WEST GROUP

From the KUA number, you determine if you belong to the EAST or WEST group. All those with KUA numbers 1, 3, 4 and 9 belong to the East group. All those with KUA numbers 2, 5, 6, 7 and 8 belong to the West group. If you are East group, then the East group directions are good for you and West group directions are not good for you. If you are West group, then West group directions are good for you and East group directions are not good for you. So take note that in using feng shui orientations, the KUA number assigns to each person four auspicious and four unlucky directions. These directions belong to either East or West groups. If you are West group, then West group directions are good for you and East group directions bring bad luck and loss. If you are East group, the East group directions are good for you and West group directions bring bad luck.

The West group directions are West, Northwest, Southwest and Northeast. The East group directions are East, Southeast, North and South.

Usually when two people of the same group marry, it is much easier to ensure both have good feng shui. If the husband and wife belong to different KUA groups and the home is not large enough to accommodate separate doors for husband and wife, use the husband's KUA direction for the main door to be facing. If it is possible to have another door to accommodate the wife's auspicious directions, it is advisable to do so. In other words, it is always beneficial to have two doors, one facing an East direction and one facing a West direction, to ensure that all residents are able to use the door most suited to them.

47 THE EIGHT DIRECTIONS

There are four lucky and four unlucky directions for every KUA number and these symbolize different types of good and bad luck. It is useful to familiarize oneself with the details of these directions as it enables us to literally select the type of good luck we want to activate simply by sitting or sleeping in a way that "taps" into our good directions.

The four good and bad directions are given special names.

The **sheng chi** direction is best. This is a growth direction and if you are able to tap your sheng chi, it brings success, a smooth life and plenty of wealth and expansion luck. Your life gets better and better. Usually if you want money and success or you want your career to take off, sit facing your sheng chi direction.

The **nien yen** direction brings love, romance and a good family life. Those wishing to have a good marriage and romance luck should sleep with their head pointed to their personalized nien yen direction. It is also a direction that makes for obedient children and helps the family attract togetherness luck.

The **tien yi** direction brings longevity and good health. When you tap this direction, you will rarely get sick. If you are feeling poorly, try tapping this "doctor from heaven" direction.

The **fu wei** direction is excellent for personal growth and development. If you want to attract study or examination luck, or to meditate, tap this direction for maximum results.

These four good directions can be energized in many different ways. You can actually be very creative in the way you use these directions and my earlier books focused on many applications of these good directions.

The four inauspicious directions begin with **ho hai,** the basic bad luck direction. Ho Hai brings mild forms of bad luck that aggravate you, but is not as serious as the other three types of misfortunes. Nevertheless it is still regarded as a negative direction that is best avoided.

The **wu kwei** direction is the "five ghost" direction, which means having bad people come into your life and disturbing you, bringing obstacles, gossip and betrayal. Usually this direction refers to problems with people, which means misfortune in relationships.

The **lui sha** direction is the "six killings" direction, which brings six types of misfortune luck. This is a bad direction indeed, which is to be avoided at all cost. Six killings means also six ways you could get seriously hurt, to an extent which can be fatal.

The worst direction is the **chueh ming** or "total loss" direction. This is the absolute worst direction and one should make all efforts to avoid this direction. It symbolizes loss of wealth, loved ones and also loss of one's good name and descendents.

It is not always possible to capture one's auspicious directions. So the idea of Eight Mansions feng shui is to strenuously avoid activating one's misfortune directions. The key therefore is to memorize one's personalized eight types of directions based on one's KUA number, and to develop the habit of always using one of the four good directions for working, sleeping, dining and all other activities of living.

SUMMARY CHARTS ON PERSONALIZED DIRECTIONS

LUCKY DIRECTIONS

Use the chart here to instantly check your auspicious directions based on your personal KUA number.

Lucky Directions						
	Wealth	**Health**	**Love & Relationship**	**Personal Growth**	**Group**	**Self Element**
Kua 1	SE	E	S	N	East	Water
Kua 2	NE	W	NW	SW	West	Earth
Kua 3	S	N	SE	E	East	Wood
Kua 4	N	S	E	SE	East	Wood
Kua 5	For Kua 5 it becomes **Kua 2 for males** and **Kua 8 for females**				West	Earth
Kua 6	W	NE	SW	NW	West	Metal
Kua 7	NW	SW	NE	W	West	Metal
Kua 8	SW	NW	W	NE	West	Earth
Kua 9	E	SE	N	S	East	Fire

UNLUCKY DIRECTIONS

You should also memorize your misfortune directions based on your personal KUA number, as it is as important to avoid inadvertently tapping into a misfortune direction.

Unlucky Directions					
Mishap	5 Ghosts	6 Killings	Life Threatening	Group	Self Element
Kua 1	W	NE	NW	SW	East	Water
Kua 2	E	SE	S	N	West	Earth
Kua 3	SW	NW	NE	W	East	Wood
Kua 4	NW	SW	W	NE	East	Wood
Kua 5	For Kua 5 it becomes **Kua 2 for males** and **Kua 8 for females**				West	Earth
Kua 6	SE	E	N	S	West	Metal
Kua 7	N	S	SE	E	West	Metal
Kua 8	S	N	E	SE	West	Earth
Kua 9	NE	W	SW	NW	East	Fire

49 THE 24 MOUNTAINS

H aving mastered Eight Mansions, you can go deeper into finetuning the selection of auspicious directions. This is done by examining the subdirections of the main directions i.e. looking at the 24 mountains (and their corresponding directions) to tell us other attributes and meanings of the subdirections. The 24 mountains reveal if a bad direction's bad influence is modified by other attributes of the 24 directions. By adding this into your Eight Mansions practice, you can select which subdirection amongst your good directions is most suitable for you.

Example: if your KUA number is 6, then your sheng chi or wealth direction is West. But you can choose W1, W2 or W3 when determining your facing or sitting direction. To see which of these subdirections is best for you, examine each of the three subdirections W1, W2 and W3. Upon doing so, you will discover that W1 is a heavenly stem direction known as Ken and its element is yang metal, so this direction is suitable if you need metal based on your birth chart. W2 is the Rooster direction and thus is excellent for those born in Rooster years. W3 is again a heavenly stem direction known as Sin and its element is yin metal.

On closer examination of the 24 mountains, you will find they are either yin or yang. You will also discover that the 24 mountains comprise the following:

1. **the 12 earthly branches**
   i.e. the animal signs. If you are a Rooster, then W2 is the best for you. Note that W1 is a yang direction and so is more suitable for a woman. W3 is a yin direction and so is more suitable for a man. This creates the balance

of yin and yang. The twelve signs of the Chinese Zodiac make up half the 24 mountain directions, so you can see that the animal sign you are born under plays a crucial role in the selection of good fortune directions. Use this information to fine-tune your use of Eight Mansions feng shui.

2. **the 8 heavenly stems**

   To see which of the stems is good for you, choose an element that produces the element of your yearly birth heavenly stem.

3. **the 4 major trigrams**

   These refer to the father, mother, son and daughter. One of these trigrams will correspond to your status within the family and when tapping your good direction, it is extra beneficial for you to check if any of these directions also coincides with your good directions.

When studying the 24 mountains, investigate them in detail and learn to use them in your selection of directions to maximize wealth and other kinds of luck. When none of the subdirections seem to apply to you in any special way, then use the yin and yang essence to fine-tune your choice of directions. This helps you to take your use of personalised Eight Mansions deeper, making it more potent and effective.

50 TWELVR BRANCHES OF THE 24 MOUNTAINS

alf of the 24 mountains are 12 subdirections that represent earthly branches. This is another name for the 12 animal signs under which all of us are born. The animal signs are the earthly branches of the year. Note that under the Chinese calendar system there are two elements in each year. One is the element of the earthly branch, the other is the element of the heavenly stem.

The animal sign that signifies your year of birth is described as your year earthly branch. The element of the year is known as its heavenly stem. Generally, when the two elements of the year are in a harmonious relationship (i.e. when one produces the other as in water with wood, or wood with fire) then the year is harmonious and auspicious. When these two elements are in discord (i.e. they are in a destructive relationship with each other) it indicates a year with problems.

For instance, in the year 2008, which is a RAT year, the element of the RAT or earthly branch is Water. But the element of the heavenly stem of the year 2008 is Earth. The heavenly stem element of Earth destroys the earthly branch element of Water. The elements of the year 2008 are thus said to indicate discord. This explanation is to tell you something about earthly branches and heavenly stems, which are used in advanced feng shui practice. Of more immediate significance however is that while using Eight Mansions you can also factor in the direction that indicates your animal sign (i.e. the earthly branch of your year of birth). These 12 animal signs are located at fifteen degree intervals around the compass. Your animal sign direction is considered auspicious for you.

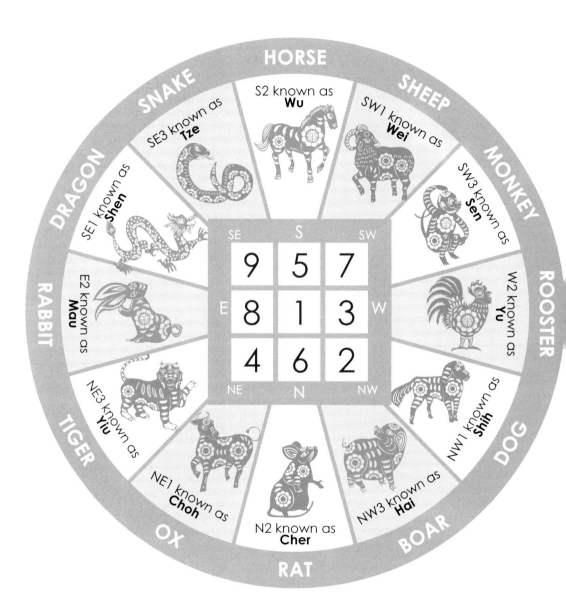

So in addition to KUA directions, we should add the extra dimension of earthly branch direction to fine-tune your choice of directions. From the illustration you can see the corresponding compass directions for each of the animal signs. Note also the name of the mountain.

These earthly branch directions indicate an additional dimension that can be factored into Eight Mansions analysis. So if you are born in the animal sign of the Dog, you know that NW1 is a good direction for you. If you are a West group person, this mountain direction will be excellent for you. If you are an East group person, the good indications of the earthly branch of this subdirection will overide any bad luck brought to you by this inauspicious West direction under the KUA formula.

At a practical level, this means that if you have no choice and have to sit facing Northwest and NW is bad for you based on Eight Mansions, then you know that if you are born in the year of the Dog, shifting your angle of sitting slightly to face NW1 would nullify any harmful luck coming towards you. If you were born in a Boar year however, then NW 3 would do the same for you. This is because NW 3 is the direction of the earthly branch that corresponds to the Boar.

This extra dimension of the Eight Mansions formula is extremely useful for those whose choice of sitting, sleeping and facing directions are limited. It expands the possibilities and the alternatives for the practitioner considerably.

51 FOUR TRIGRAMS OF THE 24 MOUNTAINS

In addition to fine-tuning based on the year animal signs, you can also fine-tune based on another set of criteria represented in the 24 mountains; these are the four trigrams that make up the 24 mountains in the secondary directions and they are placed in the Northwest, Southwest, Northeast and Southeast of the compass.

Using the Later Heaven Arrangement of the trigrams around the compass, these four directions correspond to the four component members of the family unit.

Thus:

1. the Northwest, which is signified by the subdirection NW 2, is the place of the trigram Chien which stands for the father. This direction / location benefits the father.

2. the Southwest, which is signified by the subdirection SW 2, is the place of the trigram Kun which stands for the mother. This direction benefits the mother.

3. the Northeast, which is signified by the direction NE 2, is the place of the trigram Gen (also spelt Ken) which stands for the (middle) son. This direction benefits the son.

4. the Southeast, which is signified by the direction SE 2 is the place of the trigram, Shun which stands for the (middle) daughter. This direction benefits the daughter.

This aspect of Eight Mansions overrides the East/West group lucky and unlucky directions thereby offering greater flexibility in using personalized directions.

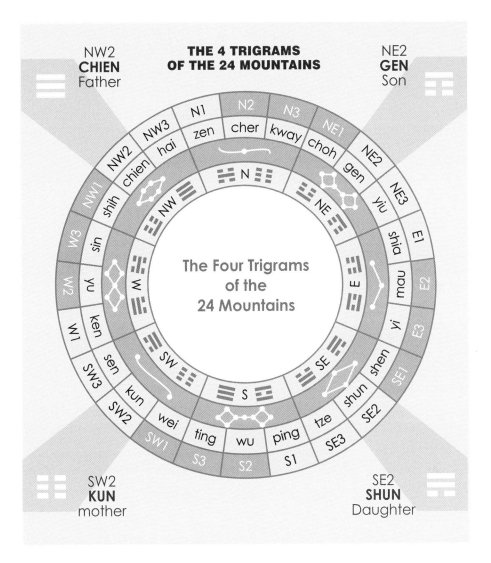

THE 4 TRIGRAMS OF THE 24 MOUNTAINS

NW2
CHIEN
Father

NE2
GEN
Son

SW2
KUN
mother

SE2
SHUN
Daughter

The Four Trigrams
of the
24 Mountains

From this diagram you can see that these four subdirections correspond to a component member of the family unit.

In practical feng shui, once you know this, you can fine-tune the auspicious corners of the home based on which member of the family you are.

Thus if your KUA number is 8 and the SW direction is good for you and you are the mother, then SW2 is definitely the direction for you. Now if you are the father, son or daughter, taking this direction means whatever good luck comes to you will also benefit the mother...

If your KUA number is 1 and the direction SE is good for you, then if you were a daughter of the family, you would fine-tune the way you sit to face the subdirection SE 2 to get a double benefit. If you are the father, mother or daughter of the family facing this direction, whatever good luck happens to you will benefit the daughter also. This part of the formula can only be used when you are considering these four directions.

Another way to use this information is when the direction is bad for you. If the direction NW is bad for you because you are an East group person but you have no choice but to face NW in your office, then if you are the father in your family, choosing NW 2 of the three subdirections of the NW will nullify any bad effect this direction brings you under the Eight Mansions formula.

So instead of facing NW 1 or NW 3, you should face NW 2, since this direction will not then be so harmful and could even bring good luck. What is required is only a very subtle shift in direction and this can easily be done with a compass and a swivel chair. This then is the huge advantage of knowing these fine points in compass formula feng shui.

52 EIGHT STEMS OF THE 24 MOUNTAINS

The last component set of directions of the 24 mountains are the eight heavenly stem directions. In the Chinese calendar system, there are really 10 heavenly stems, but in the twenty four directions of feng shui, only 8 of the stems are represented. This is illustrated below:

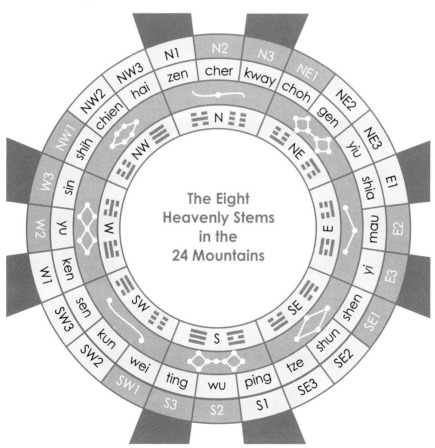

The Eight Heavenly Stems in the 24 Mountains

The heavenly stems are the first and third subdirections of the four cardinal directions North, South, East and West.

In the North, the element is water. The stems here are yang Zen (N1) and yin Kway (N3).

In the South, the element is fire. The stems are yang Ping (S1) and yin Ting (S3)

In the East, the element is wood, The stems are yang Shia (E1) and yin Yi (E3)

In the West, the element is metal. The stems are yang Ken (W1) and yin Sin (W3)

To use these directions in the fine-tuning of your application of Eight Mansions, you will need to know the element of the heavenly stem of your year of birth. Once you know that, take note of the elements above, but also note if the elements have a yin or yang aspect.

Note the ELEMENT of each of the 24 directions corresponding to the STEMS as follows:

- S1 PING is YANG FIRE
- S3 TING is YIN FIRE
- N1 ZEN is YANG WATER
- N3 KWAY is YIN WATER
- E1 CHIA is YANG WOOD
- E3 YI is YIN WOOD
- W1 KEN is YANG METAL
- W3 SIN is YIN METAL

Use the productive and destructive cycle of the elements to find out which of the stem directions are good for you and which are bad. The stem direction with an element that produces your stem element is good for you. That which has an element that destroys or exhausts your stem element is bad for you.

Next, note that yang water destroys yang fire. But yang water does not destroy yin fire.

Note also that yang wood produces yang fire. But yin wood does not produce yang fire.

So how do you determine if you are yin or yang? By noting your year of birth to determine if your heavenly stem is yin and yang. Also if you are female, you are yin, and if you are male, you are yang.

The use of the stems formula can be confusing and difficult. If you find it is not worthwhile to apply this part of the formula, you can pass on it. But facing a stem that brings luck is said to be very auspicious.

53 IMPORTANT RULE OF EIGHT MANSIONS

One of the principles of Eight Mansions which gives rise to real difficulties on a practical level arises from the sitting and facing directions that become significant in advanced feng shui practice. One of the guidelines advocated by experts focuses on two things:

1. To enjoy benevolent chi and to benefit from auspicious luck, West group people should live in West houses and East group people should live in East houses. Houses are defined as West houses when they are sitting in a West direction. Houses are deemed East houses when they are sitting in an East direction. Note that the sitting direction is the opposite of the facing direction and it is the sitting direction that defines what kind of house it is.

2. At the same time, West group people should have their main door facing a West direction and East group people should have their main door face an East direction, preferably their sheng chi direction, since this is the direction that brings success, wealth and good fortune.

In following this guiding principle, many people get confused when their houses face West, East, Northwest or Southeast.

These four directions have facing and sitting directions that belong to different groups. When the facing is East, the sitting is West. As a result, if you are an East or West group person, then only one of the sitting or facing directions is auspicious for you.

The other direction is inauspicious. As a result, the good and bad is said to cancel out and you cannot then benefit from either direction. The confusion arises when it is assumed that everyone can use their personal sheng chi direction as their facing direction and still benefit from their house sitting direction. This is of course not possible.

The West group directions are West, NW, SW and NE and the East group directions are East, SE, North and South. Confusion can arise because when your house faces East, it is sitting in the direct opposite direction which is West! The same is true of houses that face Northwest (a West direction) - they are said to be sitting Southeast, an East direction.

So it does look like that there can be a contradiction for those whose sheng chi directions are East, Southeast, West or Northwest. It would appear that in using their sheng chi direction to tap good fortune, they will be simultaneously making their house into the opposite group and bringing bad luck upon themselves. This is because both the house sitting and facing directions are equally important.

It appears that those whose KUA numbers define these four directions as their sheng chi direction simply cannot tap their sheng chi direction as their facing direction. This drawback applies to those with KUA numbers 1, 6, 7 and 9.

54

EAST & WEST GROUP AXIS DIRECTIONS

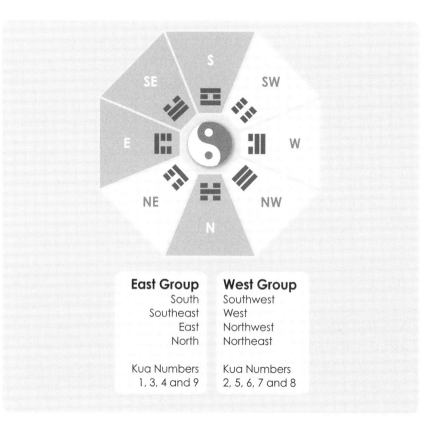

East Group	West Group
South	Southwest
Southeast	West
East	Northwest
North	Northeast
Kua Numbers	Kua Numbers
1, 3, 4 and 9	2, 5, 6, 7 and 8

If you look at the diagram shown above, you will note that the allocation of directions into East or West looks very much like the yin yang symbol. Note that amongst the East directions, North stands alone and among the West directions NE stands alone. This resembles the bit of yin in yang and the bit of yang in yin. (See the little dots in the yin yang tai chi symbol in the middle of the Pa Kua). This suggests significance to the directions North and NE.

This piece of information is significant in advanced feng shui, which goes into deeper analysis of the formulas. It does not mean that simple feng shui does not work, but when you go more advanced in your practice, you have more choices. It enhances the breadth and scope of your practice. The importance of the directions North and Northeast lie in their opposite or sitting directions. This introduces the concept of **axis directions**.

When you understand the concept of axis directions, you will realize that it IS possible for West group people to live in houses that face West and still be West houses; and for East group people to live in houses that face East and still be deemed East houses. This becomes possible when the house is facing an axis direction and there are two axis directions, one each for East and West group people.

The axis direction for East group is North/South.
The axis direction for West group is NE/SW.

You will see that North and Northeast are the two stand-alone directions in their group.

So North has access to its fellow East group directions through the opposite direction of South. This means that when you face North, you will be sitting South and vice versa. Since both are East directions, you are facing and sitting in an East group direction. So if you are East group person, then North/South axis houses are excellent for you.

Similarly, NE has access to its fellow West group directions through the opposite direction Southwest. The SW/NE axis is excellent for houses during flying star periods that belong to the West group. Hence in the current Period 8, for instance, a West group direction house is in sync with the period because the number 8 corresponds to the West direction of Northeast. In the coming Period 9 (which starts Feb 4th 2024) however, it will be East group houses that will be more favourable in terms of chi energy synchronizing with the period. That is when houses tapping into the North/South axis directions will benefit.

When your house faces either Northeast or Southwest, you will be facing and sitting in a West group direction, and if you are a West group person, a house with a SW/NE axis is excellent feng shui for you. This is one of the premier facts about Flying Star feng shui – to ensure that the house you live in is in sync not only with you personally, but more important, also in sync with the period. According to some feng shui masters, even East group people benefit from living in NE/SW axis houses during Period 8.

What then about couples who do not belong to the same group? It would seem equitable to have the house face East and sit West (and vice versa) thereby benefiting both? This solution is ideal and both parties benefit from the orientation of the home, with one reaping good feng shui from the facing direction and the other benefiting from the sitting direction.

55

THE CASTLE GATE DOOR

There is a little known gem related to Flying Star that is known as the theory of the castle gate entrance. This is a secret previously known only to advanced practitioners and it is said that this was one of the powerful secrets of one of Singapore's most famous feng shui masters of the last century, the monk Venerable Hong Choon. According to this theory, when a building succeeds in tapping the Castle Gate entrance, residents within will prosper through an entire cycle of sixty years. Many of the prosperous companies in Singapore that built buildings in the busy Orchard Road and Scotts Road areas during the Sixties show evidence of the castle gate entrance.

These buildings (or at least their entrances) are built at an angle to the main road. The Castle Gate theory requires the entrance of the building to be positioned at an angle of 45 degrees to the main road. If you visit Singapore, you will see that at the junction of prosperous Orchard Road where still stands Shaw House and the Cathay Building, two high profile head offices belonging to old money tycoons of Singapore, these buildings were built this way. The department store CK Tangs was also built this way.

The most famous and often-quoted example of feng shui magic is the way the entrance doors into the Hyatt Hotel at Scotts Road in Singapore were positioned to tap this theory. Till today, the doors into the very modern Hyatt Hotel continue to be positioned at a 45 degree angle to the main road. You only have to visit this hotel to see for yourself how it has prospered. According to feng shui folklore, the legendary Hong Choon designed the feng shui of the Hyatt. It is said that after this master repositioned the door to tap the Castle Gate method, Singapore's Hyatt Hotel's fortunes have never looked back.

In addition, it was also believed that the monk added a yang water feature to make the Castle Gate more auspicious. Water here is not still. It is not yin. It is yang and moving. Thus fountains were added to strengthen the Castle Gate feature of Hyatt hotel. The water feature was added because the Hyatt hotel building had originally been built without the benefit of feng shui advice as a result of which business had suffered. The master was thus called in later when business was so bad the owners had little choice but to succumb to local advice. When the hotel was first built, both the building's orientation and its doors had faced the main road directly. So when only the glass door directions (and not the whole building's orientation) could be changed, it was feared the Castle Gate created was not strong enough. Hence the addition of the yang water feature.

When the Castle Gate is blocked for some reason, either by a large pillar or tree, the chi in front of the door is said to be negatively disturbed. In such a situation, additional yang energy is needed to pull in the chi from outside into the building. Having a revolving door at the Castle Gate does this. This feature is said to be extremely auspicious when the flying stars at the entrance into the building are also auspicious. The revolving gate activates and churns up the benevolent chi.

Note that to cast the Flying Star chart, one takes the facing direction as though the building faces the main road, even though the door may have been angled at 45 degrees to the road to tap the Castle Gate direction. This is a very important fine point to remember.

56 CASTLE GATE DOOR DIRECTIONS

I n the old days, veteran practitioners of feng shui were especially fond of erecting Castle Gate doors as this was one of the surest and fastest ways of attracting financial good fortune. The theory of the Castle Gate Door is closely allied to Flying Star feng shui. Here the main door into the building or home is angled to capture success and wealth luck for residents within. Conventional Flying Star uses period charts to unlock the pattern of chi to attract prosperity luck. When you can also incorporate Castle Gate theory into your feng shui, it will bring you to even greater heights of prosperity.

If you do not have a good mountain star supporting you, or your facing direction is somehow affected by some obstacle in the environment, you can tilt your door and make it a Castle Gate door to bring prosperity. Here are the detailed door directions of the authentic Castle Gate door. Castle Gate theory is based on the sitting and facing directions of houses.

Please note that in every house, there are two possible directions that bring in the auspicious energy of the Castle Gate. There is the main auspicious energy and the secondary auspicious energy. The two directions for each FACING direction of house are as follows:

House facing South.
The 2 directions of Castle Gate are SE and SW.

House facing North.
The 2 directions of Castle Gate are NW and NE.

House facing West.
The 2 directions of Castle Gate are NW and SW.

House facing East.
The 2 directions of Castle Gate are NE and SE.

House facing Northeast.
The 2 directions of Castle Gate are EAST and NORTH.

House facing Southwest.
The 2 directions of Castle Gate are SOUTH and WEST.

House facing Northwest.
The 2 directions of Castle Gate are NORTH and WEST.

House facing Southeast.
The 2 directions of Castle Gate are SOUTH and EAST.

Facing **South**, the auspicious castle gate should face **Southeast**. This is because the combination number between South and Southeast based on the original Lo Shu number is 9/4. The SE door forms a HO TU combination with the facing direction of the house ie South. The secondary direction of **Southwest** is thus less auspicious.

Facing **North**, the auspicious Castle Gate should face **Northwest** because the combination number between North and Northwest based on the original Lo Shu number is 1/6. This forms the lucky HO TU combination. Here the secondary direction is **Northeast**.

Facing **West**, the auspicious Castle Gate should face **Southwest**. This is because the combination number between West and Southwest based on the original

Lo Shu number is 7/2. This forms the auspicious HO TU combination. So, the secondary direction is the **Northwest**.

Facing **East**, the auspicious Castle Gate should face **Northeast**. This is because the combination number between East and Northeast based on the original Lo Shu number is 3/8. This forms an auspicious HO TU combination. So the secondary direction is the **Southeast**.

Facing **Northeast**, the auspicious Castle Gate should face **East**. This is because the combination number between Northeast and East based on the original Lo Shu number is 8/3. This forms the HO TU combination. The secondary direction is **North**.

Facing **Southeast**, the auspicious Castle Gate should face **South**. This is because the combination number between Southeast and South based on the original Lo Shu number is 4/9. This creates the lucky HO TU combination. Here the secondary direction is the **East**.

Facing **Southwest**, the auspicious Castle Gate should face **West**. This is because the combination number between Southwest and West based on the original Lo Shu number is 2/7. This creates a lucky HO TU combination. The secondary direction is the **South**.

Facing **Northwest**, the auspicious Castle Gate should face **North**. This is because the combination number between Northwest and North based on the original Lo Shu number is 6/1. This forms the HO TU combination. The secondary direction is the **West**.

The theory of Castle Gate was used during the old days to ensure the prosperity of whole villages. In those days, there would usually be only one main gate, which would the only entrance into, and exit out of, the village. It was important to ensure the village gate had good feng shui as it affected the feng shui of the whole village. At the same time, there would also be only one source of water supply. To make sure the water was in a good location to bring the best wealth and prosperity luck to the village, they would usually place a well at the front of the gate. The energy of the well (water) would then flow into the village. For example, if the whole village was facing Southwest, they would build the gate to face West and place a well in front of it. If they could not get the main wealth direction, then they would use the secondary direction.

It is necessary to ensure that the energy coming from either the main auspicious Castle Gate direction or secondary direction is gentle, good and fresh. There should not be any shar chi, stagnant and slow energy facing the Castle Gate.

In the Pa Kua, there are 24 directions also known as the 24 mountains. Each direction has its own main and secondary wealth directions and it is necessary to fine-tune the directions and be as accurate as possible. The following is the list of potential Castle Gate door directions (main and secondary) for each of the 24 mountain directions.

Facing N2 – Main wealth direction is NW2 and secondary direction is NE2.
Facing N1 – Main wealth direction is NW1 and secondary direction is NE1.
Facing N3 – Main wealth direction is NW3 and secondary direction is NE3.

Facing NW1 – Main wealth direction is N1 and secondary direction is W1.
Facing NW2 – Main wealth direction is N2 and secondary direction is W2.
Facing NW3 – Main wealth direction is N3 and secondary direction is W3.

Facing W2 – Main wealth direction is SW2 and secondary direction is NW2.
Facing W1 – Main wealth direction is SW1 and secondary direction is NW1.
Facing W3 – Main wealth direction is SW3 and secondary direction is NW3.

Facing SW1 – Main wealth direction is W1 and secondary direction is S1.
Facing SW2 – Main wealth direction is W2 and secondary direction is S2.
Facing SW3 – Main wealth direction is W3 and secondary direction is S3.

Facing S2 – Main wealth direction is SE2 and secondary direction is SW2.
Facing S1 – Main wealth direction is SE1 and secondary direction is SW1.
Facing S3 – Main wealth direction is SE3 and secondary direction is SW3.

Facing SE1 – Main wealth direction is S1 and secondary direction is E1.
Facing SE2 – Main wealth direction is S2 and secondary direction is E2.
Facing SE3 – Main wealth direction is S3 and secondary direction is E3.

Facing E2 – Main wealth direction is NE2 and secondary direction is SE2.
Facing E1 – Main wealth direction is NE1 and secondary direction is SE1.
Facing E3 – Main wealth direction is NE3 and secondary direction is SE3.

Facing NE1 – Main wealth direction is E1 and secondary direction is N1.
Facing NE2 – Main wealth direction is E2 and secondary direction is N2.
Facing NE3 – Main wealth direction is E3 and secondary direction is N3.

When you are not sure of the facing direction of your house you can still find the main wealth direction based on the surrounding environment. Thus if your house has one of the following features, you can tilt your door to face that direction.

1. A busy road where plenty of people walk in and out.
2. When there is the entrance to a river, a canal or waterway.
3. When there is an entrance facing a valley or exit from a valley.
4. When a single river splits into 3 small rivers in front of you.
5. When your house faces a big lake or mining pool.
6. When there is a curve of a river and it seems to be embracing your house.

7. When on the left and right there is a pond or lake.
8. When you have a round shaped mountain in front.
9. When both sides of your house has a tall building, a nice mountain or a pagoda.

REVITALISING YOUR CASTLE GATE DOOR

When the period changes, you need to renovate your Castle Gate to welcome the new energy. For example, if during Period 7 you have tilted your main door to become a Castle Gate door you need to revitalize the energy. Because we have entered into Period 8, the energy of your Castle Gate has declined and if you continue to use the door, <u>it will bring bad luck</u>. You need to renovate the Castle Gate to welcome the new energy of period 8 in order to continue to enjoy prosperity luck. When you revitalize your Castle Gate door, you will instantly enjoy a spurt of good fortune. This is done by knocking down the door and then rebuilding it!

57 FEATURES AT FRONT OF BUILDING

Please note that to obtain the best possible influences from the Castle Gate, it is beneficial to add decorative features in front of the building that resemble three joss sticks (please note it has to be three, not two or one). These are said to be offerings to the God of Wealth. In Singapore, clever Chinese tycoons who believe in feng shui place three round conical shaped structures in front of their building that resemble giant joss sticks – except that these structures are actually giant flower pots decorated with live orchids and other foliage plants.

Having these features is very different from having three pillars as part of the front of the building. When you have three pillars, they are described as keeping the mouth of the building perpetually open. Unable to close, the entrance of the building then resembles a mouth that cannot shut – so all the money rolls away! So do away with three stand-alone pillars at the front of the building. They do not represent good feng shui. Instead, place decorative features that stand alone and are not part of the building.

A popular method of activating the front of the building with auspicious objects thereby strengthening the Castle Gate door is to place weatherproof statues of the three star Gods Fuk, Luk and Sau on the roof facing the direction of the house. When I visited Shanghai, I took a tour of many of the grand old houses of this wonderful and fast-growing city and discovered several examples of old homes that used this method to activate the front parts of their homes.

58 AUSPICIOUS SW/NE EARTH AXIS

A little known tip given in a feng shui almanac recommends that one of the best directions for the main entrance is one that faces just off the SW/NE axis. This is an excellent axis direction for a main entrance for the current period of 8 and it also simultaneously taps the Castle Gate theory. This is known as the "earth axis". In the texts, these directions are described in accordance with their names *wei* and *choh.*

Wei is actually the mountain direction SW 1, while *choh* is the mountain direction NE 1. This direction is doubly auspicious for people who belong to the West group of KUA directions. If you can tap either of these directions SW1 or NE 1, try also to simulate inward flowing water as this is one of the best ways of accumulating wealth. Make sure the water flows inwards. When water flows outwards in full view of the main entrance, it signifies financial loss.

This is an excellent way to orientate houses for Period 8 and in this connection, it is better to sit Northeast and face Southwest than the other way around. To ensure prosperity through the twenty year Period of 8, you should also create a substantial and meaningful water feature in the front of the Southwest location. This water feature should be directly facing your main door.

In doing this, you will also be facing what feng shui experts refer to as the INDIRECT SPIRIT of the period (more of this later). According to ancient texts on Flying Star, when there is water in the indirect spirit, there will be great wealth attracted to the abode.

For those of you keen on maximizing your feng shui luck, look for, or build a house that faces Southwest and sits Northeast. Then make sure you orientate the house to face Southwest 1 so that for good measure the auspicious water star 8 will also be at the front of the house in the Southwest direction.

WATER IN FRONT OF A SW1 FACING DOOR

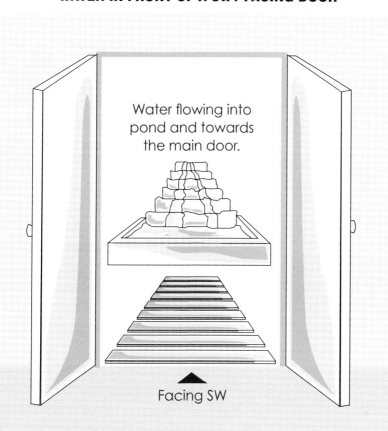

Water flowing into pond and towards the main door.

Facing SW

59 AUSPICIOUS FLOW OF WATER

For yang dwellings, you can apply the water formula to the way water flows around your home as a means of activating and attracting wealth luck. What you need to remember is that for directions referring to the heaven plate, we must add 7.5 degrees to readings taken from a standard western-style compass. This adjusts for the difference in reading between the earth plate and heaven plate, and adding 7.5 degrees makes it a heaven plate reading. This way, amateur practitioners wishing to use the water flow guidelines contained in the Three Harmony water formulas, which are reproduced here, can do so.

First, take the facing direction of the house. Remember that this is usually the same as the facing direction of the main door unless the main door is facing a garage or a side road and is blocked. So it is important to determine the facing direction of the house correctly.

For all houses and buildings with a facing direction East 1, North 1, East 2, North 2, West 1, West 2, South 1, South 2, i.e. all the cardinal directions 1 and 2, the water should flow past the front of the house from left to right i.e. in a clockwise direction, with the direction taken from inside the house facing out.

Note that this applies to all houses facing a cardinal direction, but the fine-tuning is that the house should not be facing any of the third subdirections. In such houses, the prosperity is yang prosperity and the source of the wealth comes from the men of the family.

For all houses and buildings with a facing direction Northwest 2, Northwest 3, Northeast 2, Northeast 3, Southwest 2, Southwest 3, Southeast 2 and Southeast

3, water should flow past the front of the house from right to left i.e. in an anti-clockwise direction.

Once again, note that this applies to all houses facing a secondary direction, but the fine-tuning is that the house should not be facing any of the first subdirections. In houses with this kind of facing direction and this kind of water flow, what flows is yin prosperity and the source of wealth comes from the women of the family.

YIN PROSPERITY

YANG PROSPERITY

Most auspicious for house/ main doors that have the following facing directions:

1. ting / wei (S3 / SW1)
2. kun / sen (SW2 / SW3)
3. sin / shih (W3 / NW1)
4. chien / hai (NW2 / NW3)
5. kway / choh (N3 / NE1)
6. gen / yiu (NE2 / NE3)
7. yi / shen (E3 / SE1)
8. shun / tze (SE2 / SE3)

Most auspicious for house/ main doors that have the following facing directions:

1. ping / wu (S1 / S2)
2. ken / yu (W1 / W2)
3. zen / cher (N1 / N2)
4. chia / mau (E1 / E2)

DRAGON GATE WATER FLOW

In addition to the flow of water past the front of the house, there is another principle that governs the flow of water coming into the house and going out of the house i.e. the incoming and exit directions of water. This is known as the Dragon Gate Water Flow, which has different guidelines for yin and yang dwellings, and is based on the sitting direction of the house. (Please note that the Dragon Gate Water Flow is different from the Water Dragon formula.)

To create Dragon Gate water, it is necessary to determine the sitting direction of the house. From the sitting direction, you determine the trigram of the house. Please take directions carefully, since the formula is based on the 24 mountains and refer to segments of only 15 degrees, which means one has to be careful to ensure a correct reading of directions. Also remember that all references to the 24 mountains here refer to the Heaven Plate, so adjustments must be made by adding 7.5 degrees to any reading taken with a compass that measures Magnetic North. This is because the Heaven Plate measures True North, and not Magnetic North.

The Dragon Gate Water Flow is summarized as follows:

1. Chien House sitting Northwest — water should flow in from the Northeast or the South and flow out in an East 1 direction. It can also flow out in a SW or West direction.

2. Kan House sitting North — water should flow in from the Southwest and flow out in an SE2 direction. Water can also flow out in an East or NW direction.

3. Ken House sitting Northeast - water should flow in from the East or West and flow out in a SW 2 direction. Water can also flow out in a North or SE direction.

4. Chen House sitting East - water should flow in from the South or Southwest and flow out in a SW 2 direction. Water can also flow out in a North or SE direction.

5. Sun House sitting Southeast - water should flow in from the West and flow out in a N 1 direction. Water can also flow out in a South or Northeast direction.

6. Li House sitting South - water should flow in from the Northwest and flow out in a NE 2 direction. Water can also flow out in a West or SW direction.

7. Kun House sitting Southwest - water should flow in from the South or North and flow out in a NE 2 direction. Water can also flow out in a Northwest or East direction.

8. Tui House sitting West - water should flow in from the North or Southeast and flow out in a NE 2 direction. Water can also flow out in a Northeast or South direction.

In feng shui, it is necessary to establish a very clear distinction between the flow of water and the presence of bodies of water. Since water makes up such an important part of the practice, there are many old texts exclusively devoted to analyzing the impact of water and water flows on the feng shui of houses.

There are different ways to approach water feng shui, but in the context of modern day situations, unless you own a country estate with big tracts of land, extensive use of water feng shui is beyond many of us, especially for those of us living in apartments. Thus I prefer to focus on the benefits to feng shui of using small water features rather than depending on large water flows. Hence I would suggest that you focus on water as applied according to Flying Star feng shui.

Using Flying Star in conjunction with the symbolic principles relating to water, it is possible to create awesome wealth luck without having to worry about the Dragon Gate method. Also, in today's environment, there are many different varieties of water features that are available at inexpensive prices and these are excellent for use in activating water chi indoors.

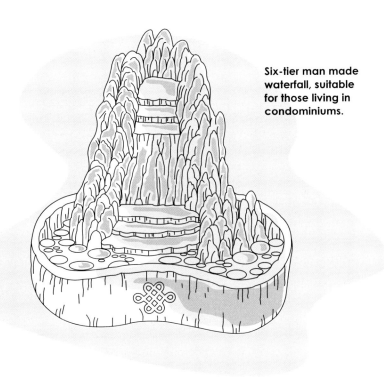

Six-tier man made waterfall, suitable for those living in condominiums.

61 PERIOD CHANGES IN FLYING STAR

Cycles of periods introduce a time dimension to feng shui. Each complete cycle lasts 180 years and each cycle is made up of three periods - the Upper, Middle and Lower periods. Each period comprises 60 years, subdivided into three subperiods lasting 20 years each. Each cycle of time comprises 9 periods of 20 years each.

(Thus 9 X 20 = 180). You may ask why nine periods? This is because there are nine numbers in the Lo Shu square on which Flying Star feng shui is based.

In each of the 20 year periods, there is a reigning number. Each assigned number, from 1 to 9, represents a period, and this number exerts great significance and influence during the period over which it rules. In its own period, the ruling number is supreme. Each 20 year period has its own Period Lo Shu chart, where the reigning number of the period is the center number.

This is referred to as the Period's Base Lo Shu Square in Flying Star feng shui.

We are presently living in the Period of 8. This period officially started on 4th February 2004. Since Period 8 is still "young", many buildings in existence were probably built during the previous period of 7. These buildings are described in feng shui as having lost most of its chi energy with the change of period. This always happens when there is a change of period.

Old energy gives way to new energy and mankind must revitalize all man-made dwellings to ensure that chi within their dwellings stay alive, fresh and in sync with the changing energy of time changes. The practice of feng shui thus includes the need to be up to date and in sync with period changes of chi energy.

But time is not measured only in twenty year periods. Changes of chi energy occur also on an annual basis and energy likewise changes each year. These changes are reflected in the annual flying star chart which must therefore be analyzed at the start of each Hsia calendar year which begins not on the lunar New Year day but instead on 4th February each year. This is the day of Spring each year, popularly referred to as the day of the *lap chun*.

Subtle changes in energy also take place monthly, so there are monthly charts which can be drawn up to reveal the way good and bad energy moves around the home.

When the feng shui month, year and 20-year charts of dwellings are studied, one will have a very precise picture of how the chi energy - its good energy and its afflicted energy - moves within the dwelling in any particular month. Knowing how to read monthly and annual energy and how to take care of the afflictions while enhancing the good fortune sectors usually makes up a large part of feng shui practice, especially formula feng shui, as this updates the energy of space in a very efficient way.

62 PERIOD LO SHU SQUARES

Each 20 year period has its own Period Lo Shu derived by placing the period reigning number in the center of the nine sector grid. From this, the remaining numbers of the square can be allotted their "place" in the grid. This placement is based on the sequence of numbers in the original Lo Shu square.

This sequence is often referred to as the flight of the stars, and the sequence of this flight of numbers makes up a sequential movement of numbers that unlocks the secrets of the Flying Star natal chart. Learn this sequence, since you will meet up with it frequently when you chart the flying stars of buildings. For now, let us look at three things:

- the original Lo Shu square, with 5 in the center.
- note the flight of its numbers i.e. where the 6, 7, 8 and so on are placed.
- then see how to derive a period 7 Lo Shu chart with 7 in the center using the same sequence.

ORIGINAL LO SHU SQUARE   **PERIOD 7 BASE CHART**

The ORIGINAL LO SHU SQUARE is a nine-sector grid with numbers 1 to 9 placed in the arrangement where any three numbers vertically, horizontally and diagonally add up to 15, the number of days that make up one cycle of a waxing or waning moon. Hence the Lo Shu is the basis of all time related feng shui formulas. Note the following:

- the number 5 is in the center
- the next number 6 is in the Northwest
- the number 7 is in the West
- the number 8 jumps across to the Northeast
- the number 9 is in the South... and so on
- each successive ascending number is in a new grid
- look at the five elements of each grid
- remember directions/numbers/elements

When you have become thoroughly familiar with the original Lo Shu square, it becomes easier to understand the placement of the numbers 1 to 9 in the nine squares that make up the grid once the center number is identified. It is important to remember that the numbers and elements associated with each number in this original square continue to hold when we study new charts created. For example, 9 is always fire, 1 is always water and so forth. Similarly, the base element of the SE sector is always wood, of NW is metal and so forth. So look carefully at the original Lo Shu square and know it well. It is the key to time cycles of feng shui.

63 THE MOVEMENT OF THE LO SHU NUMBERS

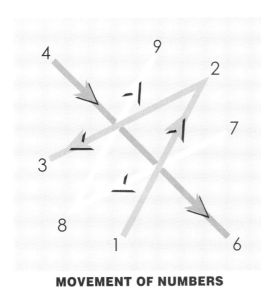

MOVEMENT OF NUMBERS

THE FLIGHT OF THE NUMBERS shown here is the way the numbers move. Starting from the center number 5, notice the next number 6 has moved to the NW... this is referred to as the flight of the star numbers. The old masters looking at this flight realized that it formed the powerful symbol of the Nine Kings. This is also the sign of the Sigil, found in Hindu as well as Jewish traditions. This sign is believed to be a powerful protective sign, which can be worn as an amulet that protects against premature death.

In Flying Star feng shui, this sign is important as an easy way of remembering how the numbers are placed around the nine-sector grid. Follow the arrows shown here. Note that the numbers here fly in an ascending fashion with the numbers getting higher from 5 to 6 to 7 and so forth. Later you will see that in flying star natal charts, these numbers can also fly in a descending order.

The PERIOD 8 LO SHU SQUARE shown here is the Base Chart of numbers of the current Period of 8. This is the base chart of all houses and buildings constructed or renovated during the period of 8, between February 4th 2004 and February 4th 2024.

This is referred to as the Period 8 chart. Note the center number is 8 and the next higher number 9 is in the Northwest.

This follows exactly the same sequence of the original Lo Shu square that had 5 in the center. All other numbers from 9 to 1 to 2 to 3 to 4 and so forth are placed in the grids in exactly the same sequential flight as the in the original Lo Shu square. Work this out in your head.

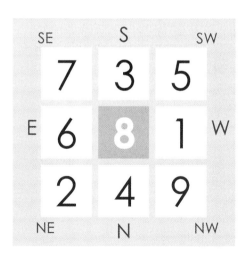

Once you know the sequence of how the numbers move, you will be able to create your own chart for all the nine periods of the whole cycle of 180 years. All you need is the center number. With this center number, all other numbers are placed in the other sectors in exactly the same sequence as in the original Lo Shu square. This is the key to Flying Star feng shui.

THE NINE PERIOD LO SHU SQUARES

S tudy the Lo Shu period squares of all the Periods reproduced on the following page. Follow the sequence in all of them and familiarize yourself thoroughly with the flight path of the numbers.

The transformations of the Lo Shu Square hold the key to unlocking all the feng shui that deals with time sequences. The key to each of the Lo Shu squares is the center number. As long as you know the center number, you can generate the Lo Shu chart of any period, any year and any month. This method holds true for the year, month, day and even hour of each day. So the charts overleaf can also double up as annual, monthly, daily or hourly Lo Shu charts.

All you need is the center number.

Every year, month, day and hour (known as the four pillars) has what is referred to as its own ruling Lo Shu number. As long as you know the ruling Lo Shu number of the year, month, day and hour, you can generate the Lo Shu chart for any particular moment in time to analyze the distribution of auspicious and inauspicious chi in any given compass sector of your house.

THE NINE LO SHU BASE CHARTS

	SE	S	SW	
	9	5	7	
E	8	1	3	W
	4	6	2	
	NE	N	NW	

	SE	S	SW	
	1	6	8	
E	9	2	4	W
	5	7	3	
	NE	N	NW	

	SE	S	SW	
	2	7	9	
E	1	3	5	W
	6	8	4	
	NE	N	NW	

	SE	S	SW	
	3	8	1	
E	2	4	6	W
	7	9	5	
	NE	N	NW	

	SE	S	SW	
	4	9	2	
E	3	5	7	W
	8	1	6	
	NE	N	NW	

	SE	S	SW	
	5	1	3	
E	4	6	8	W
	9	2	7	
	NE	N	NW	

	SE	S	SW	
	6	2	4	
E	5	7	9	W
	1	3	8	
	NE	N	NW	

	SE	S	SW	
	7	3	5	
E	6	8	1	W
	2	4	9	
	NE	N	NW	

	SE	S	SW	
	8	4	6	
E	7	9	2	W
	3	5	1	
	NE	N	NW	

66 REIGNING NUMBER OF PERIODS

O nce you know the reigning number that rules the period, you can draw up the base flying star chart of all dwellings - buildings, houses, cities, and even countries - for feng shui analyses. The reigning number of every twenty years gives its name to that period. For example, we have just finished the twenty years of Period 7 and we are now in Period 8.

Because the origins of these numbers lie in the mysterious mathematical arrangements of the Lo Shu and is influenced by the Pa Kua, it is widely believed that this number, i.e. the number that "rules" the period, is extremely auspicious during the period. The number 7 represented prosperity and wealth during its period, but that period is now over, so the number 7 has reverted to its original character, which is violent and negative. So from 2004 until 2024, the number 7 is a number which brings misfortune which manifests as violence and robbery.

When you study time dimension feng shui, you must take note of this and start to investigate the things that need to be done to protect your feng shui. We all need to be protected from the number 7's violent nature now that we are no longer in Period 7.

67   THE PERIOD OF 8

This period began on February 4th 2004 and lasts for 20 years. The number 8 corresponds to the direction Northeast, represented by the Trigram KEN. Its element is earth and it signifies keeping still, like the mountain. KEN personifies the young man and is associated with the end of everything and the start of a new beginning. In feng shui, the number 8, a very auspicious white number, represents "present prosperity".

In this period, all those who belong to KUA 8, or whose house numbers are 8 will benefit significantly. In terms of numbers, the combination of 7 with 8 signified great good fortune during Period 7 because at that time it meant "current" as well as "future" prosperity. But as soon as we entered Period 8, these numbers became weak. Instead, we should now be looking at combinations of double digit 8s as well as combinations of 8 and 9. These two numbers combine fire and earth and are most auspicious because fire produces earth.

Those still living in Period 7 houses must try to undertake renovations to their homes to change to Period 8. If this is not possible, they must suppress the evil influence of the 7 star with the presence of water. Hence in Period 8, houses need water features not only to attract wealth luck but also to suppress the violent 7 star.

LUNAR & SOLAR CALENDARS

The Chinese have two calendars - the lunar and the solar calendar.

THE LUNAR CALENDAR

This is the calendar most English-speaking Chinese are familiar with. In this calendar, the New Year date changes between January and February from year to year. It is necessary to check the hundred year calendar to see the start of each New Year. This is the calendar used in the celebration of Chinese New Year, in the determination of one's animal year of birth, in our investigation of life destiny analysis, and in determining the heavenly stem and earthly branch elements of our year of birth. When we use the KUA or Eight Mansions formula, we use this lunar calendar, and any adjustments to our lunar year of birth uses this calendar.

THE SOLAR CALENDAR

Flying Star feng shui uses the solar calendar. This is also known as the Hsia calendar and differs from the lunar calendar in that the start of each New Year under this calendar is Feb 4th (there is a margin of error of one day in certain years, but 4th Feb is a safe day to use as the changeover date from year to year). This corresponds to the start of spring in the year, also known as the day of the *lap chun*. Flying Star annual and monthly periods are based on this solar calendar, and the Lo Shu numbers of each year and month are expressed on the basis of this calendar. Thus when we speak of Flying Star annual and month charts, it is important to note that our equivalent western calendar dates use this calendar to make the date conversions.

LO SHU NUMBERS OF DIFFERENT YEARS

REIGNING NUMBERS FOR SOLAR CALENDAR YEARS 2000 to 2025

YEAR	Reigning number	YEAR	Reigning number	YEAR	Reigning number	YEAR	Reigning number
2000	9	2007	2	2014	4	2020	7
2001	8	2008	1	2015	3	2021	6
2002	7	2009	9	2016	2	2022	5
2003	6	2010	8	2017	1	2023	4
2004	5	2011	7	2018	9	2024	3
2005	4	2012	6	2019	8	2025	2
2006	3	2013	5				

The chart above enables anyone to work out the Lo Shu square of any year. To obtain the Lo Shu chart for any particular year, look for its equivalent Lo shu number. Remember that this is the reigning number that goes to the center of the chart, and all other numbers are then filled in, in accordance to the sequential flight or movement of numbers disscussed earlier. It is possible to see which number goes in which direction grid. E.g. In 2008 the annual flying star chart has 1 in the center and the chart is generated using this as the center number.

SE	S	SW
9	5	7
E 8	1	3 W
4	6	2
NE	N	NW

Note: The dates may have a variation of one day plus or minus. The above is the summary of the 10,000 year calendar which can be consulted for more accurate analysis of the luck according to different months of the years. First, check the animal earthly branch ruling in the year, then use the reigning numbers of each month to derive the flying star chart for that month.

70 LO SHU NUMBERS OF DIFFERENT MONTHS

The table on the following page is the reigning Lo Shu numbers of the different months which you can use to generate the flying star chart for any month of any year. Determine the animal sign that rules in the year under investigation. For instance, the year 2008 is the year of the Rat. So the reigning number for the first month starting 4th February and ending March 6th is the number 8. You will note that the reigning number for year 2008 in the year of the Rat is the number 1, so to obtain the annual and month chart for the first month of the year 2008, you combine the annual with the month chart.

So the combined numbers of 1 and 8 rules the first month's energy of the year 2008. So in the first month of 2008, the center part of dwellings is very auspicious as the combination of 1/8 is auspicious being both white numbers. Both 1 and 8 are also lucky numbers. You can draw out the chart for that month and start to study the number combinations to determine the luck of each of the other sectors of your house in the first month of the year 2008.

REIGNING NUMBERS FOR
THE SOLAR CALENDAR MONTHS IN VARIOUS YEARS

START OF MONTH	YEAR of RAT, RABBIT, HORSE & ROOSTER	YEAR of DOG, DRAGON, OX & SHEEP	YEAR of TIGER, BOAR, SNAKE, & MONKEY
FEB 4TH	8	5	2
MARCH 6TH	7	4	1
APRIL 5TH	6	3	9
MAY 6TH	5	2	8
JUNE 6TH	4	1	7
JULY 7TH	3	9	6
AUGUST 8TH	2	8	5
SEPT 8TH	1	7	4
OCT 8TH	9	6	3
NOV 7TH	8	5	2
DEC 7TH	7	4	1
JANUARY 6TH	6	3	9

71 ANNUAL AFFLICTIONS

I t is important to update your feng shui annually because at the start of each year you must take into account the yearly afflictions revealed in the annual chart. These afflictions have the potential to cause a great deal of misfortune and this can be so unlucky that losses and illnesses can be fatal. Depending on what type of affliction it is, and in which sector the affliction hits, sometimes these annual horrors can cause bankruptcy, loss and even death. How severe they are depends also on your animal sign luck in any particular year. It is a good idea to update your astrological readings each year.

This is one of the motivations behind my passion for feng shui. It is simply so vital to take note of the annual afflictions, and it is also so easy that not to do so seems rather foolish. Illness, business collapses, loss of employment, accidents, sudden reversals of fortune, separations and divorces can so easily be avoided by taking the necessary precautions, because all the afflictions can be overcome with remedies.

All it requires is for you to understand the influence of annual numbers within the flying star charts each year.

Let me tell you the story of what happened at ELEMENT, my first Publisher. As those of you who have followed my feng shui books will know, ELEMENT published my big hit *The Complete Illustrated Guide to Feng Shui*. In discovering me, they discovered feng shui, and in turning the book into a hit, they in effect brought feng shui to a global audience.

In 1996 when I met them, I recall advising them to shine bright lights at their entrance area, which was placed South and also facing South. According to feng shui, when you activate the South with lights, and especially if you have an entrance there, it will bring great recognition and success. This they did and through the course of the next three years from 1996 through to 1998, ELEMENT became world-famous for their wonderful Mind, Body and Spirit books. Other publishers envied them their MBS list and indeed, they came out with stunning and beautiful colour illustrated books, and they grew enormously fast.

Alas in 1999, what is known in feng shui terms as the Five Yellow flew to the South sector and for ELEMENT this signified the beginning of the end. Since their main door was placed in the South, and it was facing South, the company bore the full brunt of the terrible five yellow. What made matters worse was they had activated the South with bright lights. Lights are fire energy, and fire produces earth. The five yellow is of the earth element. As a result, the five yellow was very considerably strengthened, and it wreaked havoc for the company and its staff. One of the senior editors discovered she had multiple sclerosis, while the Managing Director was severely hurt in a freak accident when a chandelier fell on her head at a Sales Convention. Financially, the company's backers decided to pull out and the company felt a financial squeeze so severe it would eventually cause them to fold... worse, they lost 2 million dollars worth of books when their warehouse was broken into. Everything that could go wrong did!

By the time I discovered their plight (I went down by train to check because I knew they were going through hard times) it was already November 1999. I advised them to turn off the lights and to hang metal windchimes to counter the five yellow. Metal windchimes or six gold coins are the best cures against the five yellow. For a while, things looked like they could improve and they might indeed pull through. A white knight investor came on the horizon with the prospect of injecting cash into the company. This would have helped save the company. Alas, the year changed and in 2000, the five yellow had moved out of the South and into the North. Into the South had come the Three Killings.

Sadly for ELEMENT, no one remembered to remove the large windchimes placed there. No one remembered to turn the lights back on. The result is that their auspicious South door, no longer energized by the spotlights, now lay at the mercy of the Three Killings, another annual affliction, which had flown into the South in the year 2000. ELEMENT collapsed and went into receivership that year. This is truly one of the saddest feng shui stories for me to tell because the MD of Element had by then become a great friend of mine. Happily, the ELEMENT imprint was eventually sold to Harper Collins who has since revived it. But of course, the glory days are now behind them.

A word of caution here, for the cycle has now gone full circle and the deadly five yellow visits the South again in the year 2008 – the year of the Rat!

72

THE MAJOR AFFLICTIONS

From the preceding story, anyone reading this must realize that updating your feng shui each year using the annual chart is not only important, it is a crucial part of practicing feng shui successfully, especially to protect your home against the annual afflictions and to overcome them with feng shui cures.

There are three potentially dangerous annual afflictions to take note of. These are:
- the five yellow also known as *Wu Wang*
- the three killings also known as *Sarm Sart*
- the grand Duke Jupiter also known as *Tai Sui*

I highlight these afflictions and cures during my ANNUAL FENG SHUI EXTRAVAGANZAS held in Kuala Lumpur, Singapore, and also in Europe and the United States. You can access www.wofs.com to check for times, dates and venues. I also post annual affliction warnings on www.wofs. com together with suggested cures at the start of each year so those of you who access the Internet should make it a point to use the information there to update your feng shui.

It is important to take note of the cures needed to overcome the afflictions of the year; although of course the best cure is to avoid them altogether if this is possible. When you know your bedroom is afflicted by either the *wu wang* or the *sarm saat* it really is best to move into another room for the year. This is because the cures may reduce the effect but when the affliction is in a sector that strengthens it or your furniture and interiors have symbols that strengthen

the affliction without you knowing it, then whatever cures you place may not be sufficiently effective. Further more, note that when your bedroom or front door is afflicted by any one of these afflictions, and the month and year numbers there are also inauspicious, then the danger gets considerably strengthened.

The best thing then is to move out of that room for that year when the affliction takes place, even if it means sleeping in the living room. If you really cannot do this, then all you can do is to try and use symbolic cures to reduce the impact of the affliction. It is hard to completely overcome the annual afflictions altogether. The sector that houses the main door is usually the most vulnerable to these afflictions. So when any of the affliction hits the sector where the main door into the house is located, the whole house will feel the effect of the affliction. In this instance, it is definitely advisable to look for another door to use for the duration of that year (if possible). This is because the opening and closing of the door activates the affliction. If using an alternative door is not an option, then you are left no other option but to install special feng shui cures to reduce the effect of these afflictions.

73

THE TAI SUI

Probably the least worrisome of the three annual afflictions is the TAI SUI or Grand Duke Jupiter, and the place of the Grand Duke changes every year. The Chinese regard him as the God of the Year and it is well known in Chinese families that he must be respected and must not be offended in any way, since doing so brings all kinds of misfortune. It is absolutely vital that you find out where he is residing each year. You can determine where he is from the astrology wheel below. The location of the Tai Sui corresponds to the location of the animal sign of the year. Thus in 2008, the TAI SUI is in the North corresponding with the direction of the Rat.

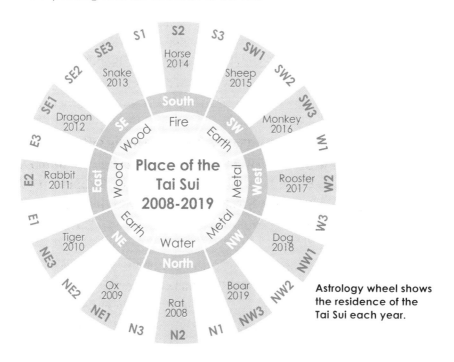

Astrology wheel shows the residence of the Tai Sui each year.

Once you know where he is located, make certain you do not incur his wrath by sitting in a direction that *faces* his direction. If you face his direction, it is construed as confronting him, and this is something you should not do. No one should face him directly when they sit or work or eat or give a speech, lead an army, start a campaign. The TAI SUI can cause havoc when one feels the full impact of his wrath.

If you confront his direction, misfortune befalls you even if that happens to be your best direction according to the KUA formula. Nor should you disturb his location with excessive noise, banging, digging or renovations. If you do, the consequences are that you could get sick, suffer losses, lose out on important deals and generally feel rather sickly. So each year, make an effort to determine his location.

The TAI SUI's locations in each of the twelve animal years of the lunar calendar follow the exact compass location of the animal year, so in 2008 he resides in the compass location of the RAT, which means the fifteen degrees defined as North 2. The astrology wheel shows the movement of the TAI SUI's location over the full cycle of the animal signs. This actually reflects the movement of the planet Jupiter in the night skies – hence TAI SUI is also known as Jupiter.

In any given year, the animal sign that is directly opposite to his location is said to be clashing with him and this brings unfortunate luck to those born under that sign. In the year of the RAT for instance, the animal sign of the HORSE clashes with the Tai Sui, so those born in the year of the HORSE should appease him.

The traditionalists usually advise that one places the image or figurine of the Pi Yao (also known as the Pi Kan or Pi Xie) inside the home in the direction of the Tai Sui. This is believed to be a very effective cure to ensure he is not offended. My advice is to always place a Pi Yao image in the home since this is an auspicious celestial creature anyway – this way, one never has to worry about offending the Tai Sui.

The Pi Yao is an effective cure for appeasing the Tai Sui.

Here is what a Pi Yao looks like. Giant images of the Pi Yao are displayed outside the Shanghai Museum and these are copies of a statue from the Tang period. In some of the old books I consulted, this creature is billed as the Pi Xie, and described as a special celestial creature used during the Tang and earlier dynasties as guardians to ward off ill luck brought by changes in time-periods. There are many different postures of this creature and you can display them in any style you wish. Just a single one is sufficient to appease the Tai Sui each year.

However, please note that Tai Sui does not always bring misfortune. If you tap into his protective shadow by sitting with him *behind* you, then you will benefit from his support all through the year. This is done by sitting facing the same direction he faces. In 2008 this means sitting with the North behind you and facing South. The only problem is that in 2008, the South is also afflicted by the THREE KILLINGS.

74 THE NASTY WU WANG

This is the affliction of the FIVE YELLOW (known as *Wu Wang* in Chinese). It is considered a very harmful affliction that in certain years can cause extreme damage to a family or a company directly hit by it. It is something everyone doing business must be aware of. The five yellow is the number five in the annual flying star chart, so it changes location each year and its effect varies in strength from year to year. It is easy to locate where this affliction is if you know how to fly the charts. It occupies 45 degrees of the compass.

In 2008, the five yellow flies to the South where it is extremely strong and potentially very harmful. This is because the South is the place of the fire, which produces earth, and the five yellow is an earth element number. In fact, it is in the South that the five yellow is strongest, so in 2008, the South is considered to be terribly afflicted.

In 2009 it flies to the North where it is still strong, as Earth controls water, the element of the North. It is always a good idea to put cures in place when its location has been determined – just in case.

When the *wu wang* occupies the sector of the house where the main door is, it becomes dangerous irrespective of which compass sector this is. Mainly because each act of opening and closing the door, or any kind of activity in the place of the *wu wang* will activate its bad vibrations, causing misfortune to befall. So do remember that when disturbed or activated, it brings calamities, accidents, illness or loss or all of these in a battalion of troubles. So if your main door is afflicted by the *wu wang*, then you should put metal cures in place.

The idea is to exhaust the chi energy of the five yellow, and since its element is earth, what is needed is metal energy in the form of brass coins and windchimes where the number 6 features strongly. The number 6 is itself a metal number, so 6 rod windchimes or 6 large coins would work well at controlling the five yellow. However, in the current period of 8, there is an even better cure and this is known as the five element pagoda. Place a brass or gold chromed five element pagoda exactly where the five yellow is located in any year and it will effectively contain its negative misfortune chi. Better yet, make a pagoda with auspicious words and with the CHIEN trigram, as this is considered much stronger and thus more effective. You need a very strong pagoda for the South in 2008.

This is the five element pagoda. Place some earth taken from your garden inside the pagoda to symbolically seal in the afflicted earth energy. It is advisable not to recycle your five element pagoda from year to year.

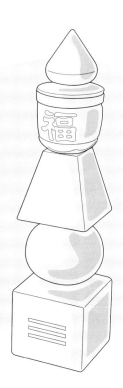

75 MORE, ON THE FIVE YELLOW

The five yellow occupies 45 degrees of the compass and its location is usually superimposed onto the traditional Lo Shu Square. Each year, locate the five yellow before you do anything else, then put cures into position. Next, take note of some important taboos associated with the five yellow.

The table below shows the place of the five yellow over the next few years starting from 2008.

In 2008, the five yellow is located in the South.
In 2009, the five yellow is located in the North
In 2010, the five yellow is located in the Southwest.
In 2011, the five yellow is located in the East
In 2012, the five yellow is located in the Southeast
In 2013, the five yellow is located in the center

In each year, everyone needs to take note of the things that must NOT be undertaken in the direction of the five yellow. These feng shui taboos are summarized below for easy reference.

- You must not dig the ground where the five yellow is. Doing so will cause you to get ill instantly.
- You must not cut down any trees where the five yellow is located. Doing so activates the affliction and you could either get sick or have an accident. Or your business will suffer a sudden setback, which can be fatal.

- You must not disturb that part of the land or house in any way with excessive noise, bright lights or activity. Do not keep dogs or pets there as this activates it.
- You must not renovate that part of the house. This involves banging and digging and it is not advisable. If you need to do renovations to parts of the house that involve the sector with the five yellow, then make certain you do not start or end the renovation in the place of the five yellow.

When disturbed, the five yellow brings loss of wealth, loss of employment, accidents, injuries, calamities, robbery and sometimes even death. The five yellow can take the form of the year or month star and when they occur in the same location at the same time, anyone residing in that part of the home will immediately get ill.

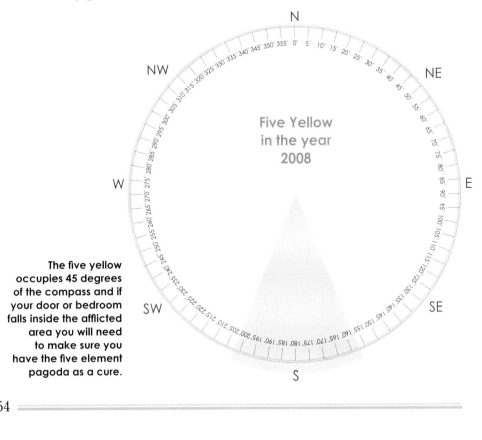

Five Yellow in the year 2008

The five yellow occupies 45 degrees of the compass and if your door or bedroom falls inside the afflicted area you will need to make sure you have the five element pagoda as a cure.

76 THE THREE KILLINGS

The three killings direction is known as the *Saam Saat* and the rule is that you must never have the Three Killings behind you at anytime. It is advisable to find out where the Three Killings is each year and then you should always confront it boldly, otherwise it sends three types of misfortunes to disturb you and make your life miserable. It is part of feng shui practice to take note of where the three killings is located every year and then take necessary precautions to ensure one is not in any way hurt by its energy.

The Three killings direction always occupies one of the four cardinal sectors North, South, East or West. So this is an affliction that covers 90 degrees of the compass. In 2008, the year of the Rat, the Three Killings is in the South. This means that during 2008, sitting with the direction South behind you can be deadly, and is definitely foolish. Instead, you should sit facing South with North behind you. This holds even when South is not one of your good directions. The rule is to always sit directly facing the direction of the Three Killings. However, in 2008, do note that the South has the Five Yellow, so it is also dangerous to sit facing South!

The idea however is to directly confront the Three Killings. Doing this is the best way to overcome its pernicious effect. When you face it, it will not hurt you, but having it behind you will hurt you a great deal and subject you to three types of misfortune including the misfortune of being betrayed and cheated. It is always more advantageous to sit directly facing the Three Killings head on. When you are planning to do house repairs and renovations, you must NOT do it in sectors that house the Three Killings. Thus in 2008, this means you should not undertake any renovations in the South part of your house.

Here is the summary of where the Three Killings affliction flies to each year. Take note of these afflicted directions during each year and follow the advice given of never having your back to this direction and never disturbing it with renovations. If you have somehow inadvertently disturbed the Three Killings, note the remedies to put into place.

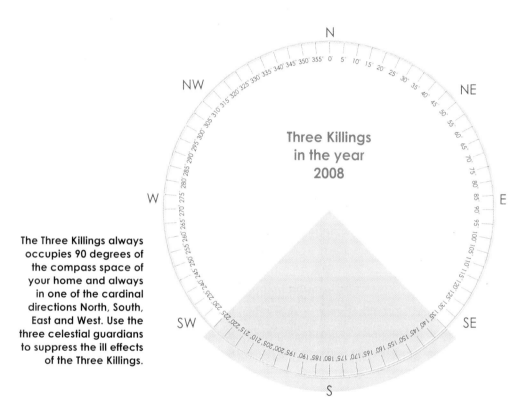

The Three Killings always occupies 90 degrees of the compass space of your home and always in one of the cardinal directions North, South, East and West. Use the three celestial guardians to suppress the ill effects of the Three Killings.

Place of the Three Killings and how to fight it:

In OX, SNAKE & Rooster years – the Three Killings is in the EAST (e.g. 2009, 2013)
Antidote: Place a curved knife in the East during these years

In Dog, Horse & Tiger years – the Three Killings is in the NORTH (2010, 2018)
Antidote: Place three large boulders in the North during these years.

In Pig, Rabbit & Sheep Years – the Three Killings is in the WEST (e.g. 2011, 2019)
Antidote: Place more bright lights in the West in these years

In Monkey, Rat and Dragon years -- the Three Killings is in the SOUTH (e.g. 2008, 2012)
Antidote: Place a large container of yin (i.e. still) water in the South to overcome.

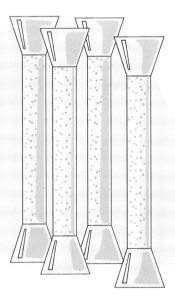

These glitter lamps are excellent cures for when the Three Killings are in the West sector of the home. You can also place the three celestial guardians.

77

HOUSE TRIGRAM FENG SHUI

There is a simple branch of Flying Star feng shui under which all houses are divided into 8 types of houses. Each house is named after one of the eight trigrams. Here the house type is determined according to the sitting direction of the house. This method is usually referred to as the Trigram House method. In this method, a chart of the house that resembles the Lo Shu chart is derived, based on its sitting direction. The chart created is then known as the Trigram chart of the house.

This concept of Trigram houses is a much easier branch of Flying Star feng shui. Trigram charts and annual flying star charts are often read together as combined charts as these offer very accurate readings of what the year holds in store for the house.

If you look at the original Lo Shu square again, you will see that each direction has a corresponding number.

To cast the Trigram chart, we first take note of the sitting direction of a house, then we see the number that corresponds to that direction in the Lo Shu square. You can see for instance that South is the number 9, North is the number 1 and so forth. Look at the numbers that correspond to all the other eight directions (in this method, the center is ignored).

To draw up the basic chart for any house, we use a compass to check its sitting direction. Note that this is the exact opposite of its facing direction. So if the facing direction is Northwest, it is sitting directly opposite i.e. Southeast.

Another way of looking at this method is to say that it is based on the sitting trigram of the house. This is because the eight directions of the compass also correspond to each of the eight trigrams. You can check this out by looking at the Later Heaven Pa Kua illustrated. As you go deeper into the different formulas, you will appreciate the significance of the Pa Kua symbol and its different attributes. Everything in the Pa Kua and the compass rings are inter-related. So in this method, houses are categorized into 8 types for purposes of analysis, with each house being named after its sitting trigram and having a Lo Shu chart where the center number corresponds to its sitting trigram number.

78

CREATING YOUR HOUSE TRIGRAM CHART

To use the Trigram House method, you have to determine what trigram your house belongs to. This requires the use of a compass to take directions.

- Use a reliable compass with directions clearly marked.
- Take readings at the main door, from inside and outside.
- Remember that it is the sitting direction you need.

When you know the facing direction of your house you can determine its sitting direction. This is the direction opposite to the facing direction. When the house faces North, it is sitting South and it is a LI house. When a house faces East, it is sitting West and is a TUI house and so forth. Each trigram house has its own ruling Lo Shu number, and from this number the chart of the house is generated based on the flight sequence of the numbers in the original Lo Shu Square. Check your trigram house from the table below.

TRIGRAM house	Facing direction	Sitting direction
A LI house	Is facing North	Is sitting South
A KAN house	Is facing South	Is sitting North
A CHEN house	Is facing West	Is sitting East
A TUI house	Is facing East	Is sitting West
A KUN house	Is facing Northeast	Is sitting Southwest
A CHIEN house	Is facing Southeast	Is sitting Northwest
A KEN house	Is facing Southwest	Is sitting Northeast
A SUN house	Is facing Northwest	Is sitting Southeast

79 USING YOUR HOUSE TRIGRAM CHART

The Trigram chart is used to track the luck of the house each year. This is because every house depending on its sitting direction will have different strengths and weaknesses in different parts. This is revealed in the TRIGRAM chart. This chart becomes a barometer of luck for the house when the annual numbers using the flying star chart of the year are added to each of the nine sectors.

Using this method you can tell the luck of different houses from year to year as they react to the year's annual charts differently. By analyzing the trigram cum annual stars chart, you will be in a good position to rearrange the layout and allocation of room usage to correspond with the annual chi energy. This is an excellent way to ensure you maximize your luck each year. To fine-tune your feng shui, you can incorporate monthly analysis into your practice. Once you are able to reach this stage of practice, you will have become quite an expert at feng shui, since you are then in a position to offer specific advice on how to avoid misfortune before it strikes and also offer remedies to overcome negative chi.

The eight Trigram charts of all houses are reproduced overleaf. These show the base charts of the houses only. To undertake the feng shui analysis, it is necessary to fill in the annual and month numbers into each grid. Only then can the charts fully reveal the luck of each sector for the year, or for the month being investigated. So identify which of these charts correspond to your house. All you need is the sitting direction of your house. It is a good idea to get familiar with the way the numbers "fly" around the charts as this is the basis of all flying star charts. Once you know the center number and you can "fly" the numbers to create the relevant chart, you will be able to practice Flying Star with great efficiency and precision.

The luck of each of the nine sectors is then read in accordance with the meanings associated with the combination of the numbers.

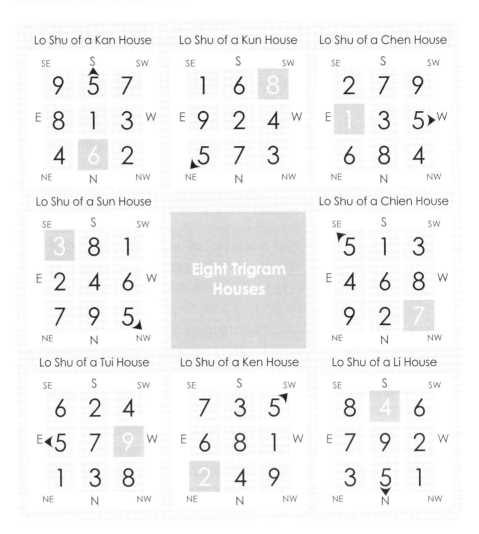

80 TRIGRAM NUMBER 1 WITH ANNUAL NUMBERS

H
ere are the indications of luck when the trigram number 1 combines with each of the nine annual numbers. When any number occurs together, the effect (good or bad) is doubled. Since the number 1 is an auspicious number, a double 1 results in what the Taoists refer to as a "double goodness" combination.

Trigram number 1 combining with annual number 1

This is an excellent double goodness combination indicating success in academic study, research, writing and creative work. There is good money luck. It is best when it occurs in the NW, West and North sectors. To enhance these numbers, and also to control any affliction that may be caused by a troublesome monthly star, use 6 rod windchimes, six coins or the five element pagoda. If afflicted by month star 5 or 2, there could be a kidney-related illness. Accidents caused by excessive drinking and alcoholic problems can also result.

Trigram number 1 combining with annual number 2

This combination can bring marriage problems and the danger of losing a child through miscarriage. There is also the danger of car accidents occurring. It is a great deal worse if this combination occurs in the SW or NE sectors of the house. Use plenty of plants to exhaust the water number 1 and place a pagoda windchime to exhaust the number 2's earth element.

Trigram number 1 combining with annual number 3

This combination brings heartache, aggravations and a great deal of stress caused by gossip, slander, misunderstandings, quarrelsome vibes and generally a breakdown in communication with many people at work and at home. There could be lawsuits and legal entanglements. It is necessary to use fire energy to exhaust the number 3 wood energy. Hence items that are red in colour are best and the best cure for this is the Laughing Buddha dressed in red robes.

Trigram number 1 combining with annual number 4

This combination attracts political luck for the year which means that all that you plan and strategize for will manifest successfully for you. There is also very good media and publicity luck. For women, there is the promise of love and romance. Those in the writing profession will enjoy excellent luck if their room is located to activate this good combination of numbers. There is good writing luck for authors. To enhance, use some water, but not too much, as excessive water leads to sexual scandal. This is a lucky combination.

Trigram number 1 combining with annual number 5

If you live in a bedroom with this combination, then the year brings you health problems; you will find it hard to withstand getting sick so you will succumb to food poisoning the common cold and all sorts of viruses more easily than others. There could also be injury caused by accidents and perhaps even the occurrence of financial and other loss. You must use the cures that overcome the troublesome 5 especially if it occurs in a SW or NE sector. In the West and NW, this combination is not so harmful. Use metal windchimes to overcome.

Trigram number 1 combining with annual number 6

There is the promise of excellent career luck. Someone will come into your life to help you. This is called the inflow of powerful mentoring luck and it is especially beneficial if this combination occurs in a NE room or a West room. Then your career will really take off in the year when you enjoy this combination. There is promotion and money luck. On the negative side, you could have more headaches than usual, especially when the month 5 or 2 flies in to disturb this otherwise fine combination. Activate by placing metal enhancers such as brass coins, windchimes, coin swords and pagoda windchimes.

Trigram number 1 combining with annual number 7

This combination brings some unsavoury violence, and any income luck that comes during the year when this combination enters your room is tainted. These numbers suggest that there will be cutthroat competition. It is important to place a water feature to control the bad vibes. When this combination takes place in a North sector you will prevail in a positive way, but when it occurs in the West or NW, you will definitely need water to overcome.

Trigram number 1 combining with annual number 8

This is an excellent combination that indicates wealth and prosperity. Unfortunately there could be misunderstandings between loved ones, siblings and good friends if this combination occurs in the East or Southeast. Business partners will then also have problems. However, when this combination occurs in the SW or NE, the luck indicated is superlative and will be made even greater when enhanced with crystals.

Trigram number 1 combining with annual number 9

This is a sum of ten combination which brings excellent career and money luck, but this is also the kind that can turn bad when the monthly 5 flies in. When that happens you could start to have eye problems. In a sum-of-ten combination, there is no need to enhance with symbolic products, but sounds and music and bright lights will be great.

TRIGRAM NUMBER 2
WITH ANNUAL NUMBERS

Here are the indications of luck when the trigram number 2 combines with each of the nine annual numbers. Note that when the number 2 occurs together, the Taoists refer to this as a "double affliction" combination. This is because the number 2 is considered the illness star.

Trigram number 2 combining with annual number 1
This combination suggests that stress develops in the marriage. There is also the danger of miscarriage, accidents, and loss of a loved one. Use a six rod metal windchime to control the negative star 2. This combination is particularly strongly when it occurs in the SW and NE, and during months when the month 5 or 2 enters to combine with these numbers, the danger of misfortune is very acute indeed.

Trigram number 2 combining with annual number 2
This is definitely not a good indication and in any year when this combination occurs in your bedroom, or worse, your front door, be prepared for illness and fatigue causing severe health problems. You will succumb to strong negative emotions and illness and accidents are a possibility. Try to overcome with several 6 rod windchimes

Trigram number 2 combining with annual number 3
When you see this combination flying into your room or where your main door is located then in that year you will experience many arguments and there will also be severe misunderstandings, the kind that lead to breaking off of ties and friendships. There is also plenty of back stabbing, legal disputes and various

other related aggravations. You can use yin water to cool tempers, but the best is to stay quiet and use silent metal energy as well as red colours to still the combination. Do not use windchimes or turn on TVs and radios in the sector that has this combination. This combination becomes particularly fierce when it occurs in the East and Southeast.

Trigram number 2 combining with annual number 4
This combination suggests that wives and mothers-in-law will burst into quarrel and fight rather bitterly. It indicates family disharmony and is especially strong when it occurs in wood and earth sectors. There are some good indications for writers and those in the journalism field. It is also a good combination for those still at school or in college. Use water to activate.

Trigram number 2 combining with annual number 5
This is an extremely inauspicious combination that spells total loss and catastrophe for the residents of the room that has it during the year when this happens. This is one of the most dangerous combinations in Flying Star, and when the month 5 flies in, anyone staying in a room or house afflicted by it can suddenly develop terminal illness. Use strong windchimes, the five element pagoda and the sword of coins to overcome. If it occurs in the South, SW or NE, it is especially dangerous. Do NOT have fire energy such as bright lights or there could be more tragic consequences such as death.

Trigram number 2 combining with annual number 6
This combination suggests a life of ease and leisure, and great power and authority during the year when you enjoy this combination. This auspicious combination is however spoilt if a 5 rod windchime is placed here. The trinity (tien ti ren) then gets activated in a negative way. Do not use windchimes. If there is sickness related to the stomach, place a red amulet here or something written with red cinnabar ink. A red robed Laughing Buddha is also good here.

Trigram number 2 combining with annual number 7

This combination suggests that the luck of the children affected by it will not be good. It also suggests problems conceiving children. There will be unscrupulous people at work who slander you and politic against you. Hang a sword of coins or place it inside your room in the place with this combination. You can also place a rooster or cockerel in the West sector.

Trigram number 2 combining with annual number 8

This combination is a sum of ten combination that brings richness and wealth to those enjoying it, but there is ill health. Although the health threat is minor, it is a good idea to establish the remedies. Use windchimes to overcome the bad health star and also place a wu lou in your bedroom on your bedside table next to where you sleep.

Trigram number 2 combining with annual number 9

This combination brings extremely bad luck. Nothing succeeds unless remedied. It is also not a good indication for children and is worse if it occurs in the South, SW or NE. To overcome the bad chi of this combination, use lots of metal energy to exhaust the 2 star and also control the 9 star with some water. Usually, to combat the illness star 2, the best is to look for an 8 Immortals wu lou made of chrome gold or brass. This will overcome all the negative vibes of this combination, but do be extra careful when the month 2 or month 9 flies in.

82 TRIGRAM NUMBER 3 WITH ANNUAL NUMBERS

Here are the indications of luck when the trigram number 3 combines with each of the nine annual numbers. Note that when the number 3 occurs together, the Taoists refer to this as a "double affliction" combination bringing misunderstandings and hostile vibes that make life incredibly uncomfortable for those residing in rooms afflicted by it. This is because the number 3 is considered the quarrelsome star.

Trigram number 3 combining with annual number 1

If your room is afflicted by this combination, there will be aggravating heartache caused by gossip and slandering. There could be lawsuits and legal entanglements. To control the effects, use water to enhance the water element. But to press down on the quarrelsome 3, you should have something red such as the Laughing Buddha dressed in red robes OR hang a red mandala painting. The annual 1 however brings victory luck.

Trigram number 3 combining with annual number 2

This is very dangerous for those in politics; It suggests that there could be lawsuits, even jail terms, so if you have this combination fly into your bedroom, it is a good idea to move out during the year these numbers are there. There will also be gossip and slander affecting you in a negative way. There is bad luck for women and a side-effect is obesity. Many feng shui masters recommend using a combination of gold and fire energy, so a red and gold mandala painting will be excellent as a remedy. Also, remember to place a brass wu lou to overcome the illness 2.

Trigram number 3 combining with annual number 3

There is gossip and slander. Quarrels abound and bad luck is doubled. Here the affliction of the number 3 star number is very serious as it is doubled. Chances of you getting robbed, cheated or burgled are also high. Use a sword of coins tied with red string. Or hang a painting that is predominantly red in colour.

Trigram number 3 combining with annual number 4

There is heartache caused by sexual scandal that leads to misunderstandings and quarrels. The use of bright lights kept turned on will dissolve much of the bad effect of this combination.

Trigram number 3 combining with annual number 5

This combination suggests there could be loss of wealth. There are severe cash flow problems. If these numbers afflict the bedroom, there will be severe financial loss. If the kitchen is here, sickness is inevitable. Do not stay in a room afflicted with this number unless you place the proper remedies in place. Exhaust the 5 with copper mountain painting and control the 3 with fire chi energy.

Trigram number 3 combining with annual number 6

This combination suggests this will be a year of slow growth. There could be leg injuries. This combination is not good for young men. Water will alleviate the situation a little bit, but you must also use the colour red, which simulates fire energy.

Trigram number 3 combining with annual number 7

This combination suggests you will get robbed or burgled. There is possibility of violence and injury from knives or guns. There could be bloodshed. Use water to overcome.

Trigram number 3 combining with annual number 8

This is not a good combination for children under 12 years of age. There is danger to limbs. Use bright lights to cure this affliction and do be careful.

Trigram number 3 combining with annual number 9

This combination brings robbery and an encounter with some unsavoury people. There could be fights and a lawsuit. Use yin (still) water to calm the situation.

Place a mandala painting with predominantly red and gold colours to help keep the number 3 quarrelsome star under control.

83

TRIGRAM NUMBER 4 WITH ANNUAL NUMBERS

Here are the indications of luck when the trigram number 4 combines with each of the nine annual numbers. Note that when the number 4 occurs, it usually brings scholastic and romantic energy, so when it occurs together it brings a "double goodness" combination. This number favours those in the writing and literary professions.

Trigram number 4 combining with annual number 1
This combination brings good romance luck but residents must beware of there being too much water as this could lead to sex scandals and affairs that lead to unhappiness and the breakup of families. But there is excellent creative and writing luck. There are feng shui masters who strongly recommend placing a Kuan Yin statue or having an image of the Laughing Buddha - when such a combination occurs.

Trigram number 4 combining with annual number 2
This combination brings illness where the problem will hurt some internal organ. The husband could be caught in a clandestine relationship. Love affairs breed problems. Use amethysts to prevent the negative fall-out of a sexual indiscretion.

Trigram number 4 combining with annual number 3
There is emotional stress due to a love relationship for those living in rooms afflicted by these numbers and there could also be sex problems. Use red chi to overcome this affliction.

Trigram number 4 combining with annual number 4
The double 4 occurring together brings excellent writing and creative luck to those who come under its influence, so in the year you have the double four enter your room, that is the time to let creative juices flow. You will also become very attractive to the opposite sex. Romance will flourish. Fresh flowers should be used to enhance the growth of romance and creativity.

Trigram number 4 combining with annual number 5
This combination suggests the possibility that you might suffer from some sexually transmitted disease. There is also the threat of breast cancer for women coming under the influence of these numbers. Overcome with a five element pagoda and other metal energy cure.

Trigram number 4 combining with annual number 6
This combination suggests some money luck, but creativity dries up. Bad luck is indicated for women, especially pregnant women. Strengthen the earth element with crystals.

Trigram number 4 combining with annual number 7
There is bad luck for those staying under these numbers who are in love. The opposite sex will cheat you. Sickness of the thighs and lower abdomen. Use water to control.

Trigram number 4 combining with annual number 8
There is excellent career luck for writers. This is a very bad combination for young children. Injury to limbs indicated. Use lights to combat.

Trigram number 4 combining with annual number 9
This is a time for preparation. It is a good combination for students. There is however a need to be careful of fire breaking out. Some water energy will be good for this sector.

84

TRIGRAM NUMBER 5
WITH ANNUAL NUMBERS

H ere are the indications of luck when the trigram number 5 combines with each of the nine annual numbers. Note that the number 5 is the *wu wang*, a much feared affliction number as it brings illness, loss and misfortune. In trigram charts, the 5 occurs in the facing palace, and this tells us that the numbers around the main door exert very strong potential of going wrong.

Trigram number 5 combining with annual number 1
This combination brings hearing problems and sex-related illnesses Use the five element pagoda to counter this affliction. Metal windchimes are also effective. However, note that the number 1 brings good competitive luck.

Trigram number 5 combining with annual number 2
This combination brings extreme bad luck. Illness contracted is likely to be serious and may even be fatal. Use metal cures such as pagodas, windchimes and coins. The most effective is the brass wu lou which is an excellent safeguard against the illness star of 2. Since it is metal, it can also keep the 5 under control.

Trigram number 5 combining with annual number 3
This combination brings aggravation caused by money troubles. There will be disputes. Those in business will experience bad luck. It is a good idea to use coins as cures, but never use windchimes as this will seriously activate the 3 leading to more quarrels. When the 3 combines with the trigram 5, there is real danger of court cases and serious litigation problems. Use red and gold to overcome the combined power of 3 and 5.

Trigram number 5 combining with annual number 4

This combination causes creativity to dry up. There is sickness and mental stress caused by misfortunes. Occupants of this sector may suffer from skin problems. Use metal energy to control the *wu wang*. Be extra careful of falling prey also to charming con-artists!

Trigram number 5 combining with annual number 5

This is a critical combination indeed as it is 5 doubled. There is extreme danger indicated. Serious illness and accidents that befall occupants could be fatal. Take care. Do not let your guard down. Move out of the room if you are able. Use a metal 6 rod windchime to overcome, as well as six five element pagodas.

Trigram number 5 combining with annual number 6

There is bad luck that leads to financial loss and monetary difficulties. Diseases related to the head region is also a danger. Place 6 coins under the carpet and hang a six rod windchime. The idea is to strengthen the 6 while exhausting the 5.

Trigram number 5 combining with annual number 7

This combination brings misfortune that leads to or arises from violence and the entrée of bad people. Arguments abound. Mouth-related illness are possible. Coins and bells make good cures. Windchimes and the five element pagoda will also work.

Trigram number 5 combining with annual number 8

There are problems related to the limbs, joints and bones of the body. It is necessary to be careful when taking part in rough or physically exertive sports. Use water to pacify this combination and hope that the lucky 8 will help to attract some good luck.

Trigram number 5 combining with annual number 9

This combination has the bad luck from the number 5 magnified, so there is bad luck all year. Do not speculate or gamble as you are sure to lose. There could be eye problems. There is danger of fire. Use water to overcome the bad luck numbers.

85 TRIGRAM NUMBER 6 WITH ANNUAL NUMBERS

T he number 6 is generally regarded as a heavenly number, bringing relatively good luck. It lacked energy during the period of 7 but in the period of 8 it is powerful once again. Here are indications of luck when the trigram number 6 combines with each of the nine annual numbers.

Trigram number 6 combining with annual number 1

This combination is auspicious as it brings good financial luck. The numbers 1 and 6 are both white numbers and they also reflect a Ho Tu combination, so it is an excellent indication of good fortune, especially for career luck during the year. High achievers in the family bring honors to the family. There could be headaches brought by excessive stress. Enhance with metal, so wear gold and hang windchimes.

Trigram number 6 combining with annual number 2

The 6 suggests great affluence and everything becoming successful. But there will also be stomach and/or womb problems for women. If the patriarch gets sick, it will be severe. No need to enhance. But control the sickness number with metal bells or windchimes. It is also a good idea to take some precautions against inadvertently falling ill.

Trigram number 6 combining with annual number 3

This combination brings an unexpected windfall. There is speculative luck although danger lurks in the shadows, so it is a good idea to be wary of "good friends". They could end up being rather double dealing. Enhance good fortune luck by wearing or displaying precious crystal gemstones.

Trigram number 6 combining with annual number 4

There will be an unexpected windfall for the women of the family. Pregnant women should however be careful. Those who benefit from this sum of ten combination should enhance their luck by displaying raw crystals, crystal points or spheres.

Trigram number 6 combining with annual number 5

There is some money luck, but it could get blocked by obstacles. The annual 5 is very powerful and it usually brings misfortune, but the metal 6 can keep it under control. It is however necessary to display the five element pagoda. There could be sickness, so use metal bells and windchimes to keep illness at bay.

Trigram number 6 combining with annual number 6

There is excellent money luck from the heavens. But too much metal can be dangerous. Do not enhance with metal any more than is necessary.

Trigram number 6 combining with annual number 7

There is competitive squabbling over money. This can lead to violent arguments involving the use of weapons. Use water to curb hot tempers and keep anger under control.

Trigram number 6 combining with annual number 8

There is wealth, popularity, prosperity and great richness. This is really an excellent combination. Those in love however could be in for a lonely period. Use the conch shell to enhance togetherness. Enhance with water and make sure you have an entrance or window in that sector. This combination brings wealth luck, so activate for wealth with water features.

Trigram number 6 combining with annual number 9

This combination brings money luck. But there could also be frustration between the generations — leading to arguments between young and old. The presence of water will reduce friction.

86

TRIGRAM NUMBER 7 WITH ANNUAL NUMBERS

There are the indications of luck when the trigram number 7 combines with each of the nine annual numbers. Note that the number 7 was very lucky for the past period, but with the change of period, this number has become violent and reverted to its evil nature. In the period of 8, the number 7 is to be feared. The double 7 was lucky before, but now it brings severe danger.

Trigram number 7 combining with annual number 1
This combination suggests extremely good prosperity luck, but competition will prove deadly. It is beneficial to use a water feature to calm down the evil eye effect. Those in competitive situations should be extra careful.

Trigram number 7 combining with annual number 2
There is the suggestion here that whatever money luck there is will quickly dissipate. Children luck is dimmed. There is also illness and robbery. Use six rod windchimes to control the bad chi.

Trigram number 7 combining with annual number 3
This combination brings grave danger of injury to limbs. Be very careful and refrain from getting into arguments with strangers. This is a combination that easily leads to litigations and problems with the authorities. Use water or bright lights.

Trigram number 7 combining with annual number 4
You could be taken for a ride by someone of the opposite sex, so do not be too trusting. Pregnant women should take care. Use water to reduce the danger of bad luck, but not excessively so, as this could also cause other dangers.

Trigram number 7 combining with annual number 5

Problems caused by excessive gossiping. Danger of poisoning or anything to do with the mouth. There is misfortune luck brought by the 5. It is really necessary to be extra watchful during the year. Use metal coins, bells or windchimes as cures to exhaust the five yellow.

Trigram number 7 combining with annual number 6

Sword fighting killing breath overcomes heaven chi. Here the situation can get out of control because we are dealing with a situation where unreasonable people clash with well meaning people. Use water to reduce the pernicious influence of 7.

Trigram number 7 combining with annual number 7

You will prevail over the competition but at great cost. Your money luck will dissipate and your sex life brings you trouble and aggravations. Use water to curb excesses.

Trigram number 7 combining with annual number 8

The combination comes under the good influence of the annual star number here, but it is a good idea to strengthen the 8 with crystal energy.

Trigram number 7 combining with annual number 9

This combination suggests a great deal of trouble that results from vulnerability to sexual advances. There is danger of fire hazards. Use earth (big boulders) to press down on the bad luck.

87

TRIGRAM NUMBER 8 WITH ANNUAL NUMBERS

The number 8 is a particularly auspicious number and brings excellent chi to any room that enjoys its presence. How good the luck is depends on the number it combines with as the annual number. Note that when the number 8 doubles, the Taoists refer to this as a "double goodness" combination which is very auspicious indeed.

Trigram number 8 combining with annual number 1
This is truly an excellent and auspicious combination that brings prosperity luck. There is career advancement. There is also added money luck. But sibling rivalry prevails. Enhance with the presence of water.

Trigram number 8 combining with annual number 2
This combination suggests that wealth creation is possible. Property and asset accumulation are all possible but there is alas, the danger of illness. Use metal energy to control sickness. The good thing here is that there is a sum-of-ten combination which always brings money luck.

Trigram number 8 combining with annual number 3
This is a very auspicious pairing as it is a Ho Tu combination bringing wealth and growth chi, but this combination is also a danger to children, so do move children away from this sector. There is danger of injury to limbs. Remedy with a display of red and fire energy.

Trigram number 8 combining with annual number 4
This suggests an overpowering matriarch. Love life of younger generation suffers

from mother and mother in law problems. There could be injury to the limbs. Use fire, or the colour red to overcome.

Trigram number 8 combining with annual number 5
There are problems related to the limbs, joints and bones of the body. It is necessary to be careful when taking part in rough sports. Use water to pacify. Here the 8 is hurt by the number 5.

Trigram number 8 combining with annual number 6
This combination is unbeatable in the SW and NE and so it brings wealth, popularity and prosperity. There will be great richness in the year. One of the best combinations in the Flying Star system. Love life could however go through a rough patch.

Trigram number 8 combining with annual number 7
This suggests residents will prevail over the competition but at a very high costs. There is money luck but there will also be some danger to life and limb. People affected by this combination should be careful. Young people should beware of over indulgence. Use water to curb excesses.

Trigram number 8 combining with annual number 8
This is a "double goodness" combination which brings excellent wealth creation luck. It is a very favourable combination indeed. No need to further enhance, although noise and yang energy will contribute to even greater good fortune.

Trigram number 8 combining with annual number 9
This combination is excellent for money luck, so it is a good idea to throw parties and have plenty of activity in this sector. The 8 gets magnified by the number 9 but the combination also brings misunderstandings between the young and older generation and these can turn nasty especially if this combination occurs in the NW of the house. Use water to calm the fire.

88

TRIGRAM NUMBER 9 WITH ANNUAL NUMBERS

The number 9 is always a magnifying number although on its own it is also an auspicious number, which suggests completion. This number has also become a number that offers future prosperity. Here are the indications of luck when the trigram number 9 combines with each of the nine annual numbers.

Trigram number 9 combining with annual number 1
This combination is good for both career and money luck, but it can turn bad when the monthly 5 flies in. There is danger of eye problems. Do not enhance.

Trigram number 9 combining with annual number 2
This combination suggests extreme illness luck. Nothing succeeds as there is danger of things getting rotten. It is also not a good indication for children. Use water plants. Also use coins or windchimes.

Trigram number 9 combining with annual number 3
This combination leads to misunderstandings and suggests you could have an unfortunate encounter with unsavoury people. There can be lawsuits and ugly fights. There is also danger of fire hazards. Use yin (still) water.

Trigram number 9 combining with annual number 4
This combination suggests a time for preparation. It benefits students preparing for important examinations during the year affected. Be careful of fire and also the use of wood or plants.

Trigram number 9 combining with annual number 5
There is bad luck all round. Do not speculate or gamble as you are sure to lose. There is danger of eye problems. There is also danger of fire. Use water to overcome.

Trigram number 9 combining with annual number 6
There is money luck in this combination but also frustration between different generations living in the same house. This can lead to arguments between young and old. The presence of water can reduce such friction.

Trigram number 9 combining with annual number 7
Troubles arise from vulnerability to sexual advances. There is danger of fire. Use earth (big boulders) to press down the bad luck.

Trigram number 9 combining with annual number 8
There is excellent luck for money and celebration. But misunderstandings between the younger and older generation can turn nasty. Use water to calm the fire.

Trigram number 9 combining with annual number 9
This combination is good or bad depending on other indications. Do not enhance.

89 ADVANCED FLYING STAR

A dvanced Flying Star makes the practice of feng shui complete as it adds the vital ingredient of periodic and time changes on the feng shui of space. Ancient texts repeatedly remind practitioners about the relevance of period cycles with each period lasting twenty years. Chi energy also has shorter-term influences that occur over annual and monthly cycles, and in addition to examining the flying star chart of your home, you also need to update your annual and monthly feng shui.

Now we investigate the effect of longer-term time influences on the feng shui of your home or office building. This requires an analysis of what is referred to as Flying Star charts. These are drawn up in accordance with a home's facing direction and according to the period when the house or building was built or last renovated, using the last renovated date as the most recent chart.

This approach highlights changing chi distribution during different time periods. It focuses on the intangible influences of environmental chi, which are expressed as numbers, or more accurately, as combinations of numbers laid out in nine squares or grids. Practitioners analyze these charts to investigate the feng shui potential of the house.

Learning advanced Flying Star feng shui means learning how to create the flying star chart and how to interpret the numbers laid out in the different sectors, and how to apply the analysis. Knowing how to enhance the good numbers to cause good fortune to materialize and how to remedy feng shui afflictions is what makes up the practice of advanced flying star feng shui.

The scope of the advanced Flying Star technique is quite awesome. It is an advanced method of investigating the luck of a house at anytime. Once you have the flying star chart of any house or building, you can scrutinize the luck of the residents very accurately; you can also forecast the ebb and flow of different kinds of the luck over time.

The forecasting dimension comes in because you can actually analyze the chart to see what the luck of the house will be in any month or year using the annual and monthly charts, and after analyzing, you can then take corrective measures accordingly. This is the method authentic feng shui masters use. How good a feng shui master is depends on how good he or she is at analyzing the numbers, activating the good numbers and diffusing the bad numbers.

Remember that although this is a compass method of feng shui, almost all the cures and enhancers that cause good luck to materialize and bad luck to be suppressed use symbolic cures based on the five elements and on the auspicious or protective nature of the symbols.

So while you are practicing compass feng shui, you are simultaneously also using symbolic feng shui. Indeed, it is knowledge of the cures and enhancers that give the oomph to the practice of advanced Flying Star feng shui.

You can use the flying star chart to investigate the luck of any corner of any room in the house. To take it further, experts also use Flying Star to analyze the luck of different parts of a city or country when they are skilled enough to do so. This is not easy to do and not within the scope this book, but it can be done.

FLYING STAR CHART OF A PERIOD 8 HOUSE
FACING EAST 1

This is what a typical flying star chart looks like. The center larger numbers are the period numbers. The little numbers at the top right of each large number are the <u>water stars,</u> while the little numbers at the top left are the <u>mountains stars.</u> Note the directions are also indicated in the chart.

90 LUCK CHANGES OVER TIME

The basic premise of Flying Star explains that good luck or bad luck i.e. harmony or disharmony in the environment, does not occur continuously or last forever. Nor do auspicious and inauspicious orientations stay so throughout one's entire lifetime. Feng shui masters point to the rise and fall of Dynasties to give credence to their conviction that there is a time element in feng shui. This time element simply cannot be ignored.

Flying Star involves annual and periodic monitoring of changes in the luck of a house by studying the influence of the earth's intangible forces. Time dimension feng shui alerts the practitioner to non-physical, invisible and inauspicious time energy. Unless countered with suitable remedies, this energy, when it is afflictive, can cause serious misfortune to befall residents. Misfortune comes as financial loss, accidents, tragedies, illness and what appears to be being in the wrong place at the wrong time.

When you read about untimely muggings, rapes, accidents and deaths in the newspapers, it should remind you that these occur because the intangible forces of the environment cause a set of circumstances to come together to cause these bad things to befall the victims. Those afflicted by intangible bad energy run the risk of coming face-to-face with unfortunate happenings. When you know Flying Star feng shui you will know how to use feng shui in a time context, making it possible for you to reduce the occurrence of accidents and misfortunes in your life. So it is really a very worthwhile skill to acquire.

Equally also, the time dimension can bring auspicious forces which cause a variety of feel good things to happen to you, and at the top of the list of these pleasant things are financial windfalls, unexpected good news or opportunities, a promotion at work, a chance meeting that brings happiness and so forth.

Good feng shui does not just bring more money – often it causes one to be in a good mood and to enjoy pleasant vibes. You will feel happier, more centered and more relaxed. Aggravations are greatly reduced and all these attributes of good feng shui occur as a result of knowing how to identify the indicators of good energy.

Always remember that happiness events and feel good energies result from good feng shui energy getting correctly activated. When the good star numbers of the flying star chart are not activated or energized with the presence of an auspicious element or image, the full benefits of the good energy simply cannot be felt.

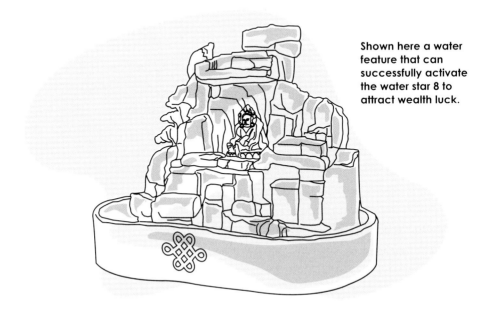

Shown here a water feature that can successfully activate the water star 8 to attract wealth luck.

CHARTING THE ENERGY OF THE HOME

Flying Star feng shui is a method of charting the energy of the home. At first it seems complex but in reality is quite easy. It is the interpretation of the numerals and their meanings that is harder to grasp and put into practice. So I advise you to begin by familiarizing yourself with the flying star chart. This is usually drawn as a nine grid square inside which are placed a set of numbers from 1 to 9. How these numbers are determined and what they mean when transferred into the different parts of your home is how Flying Star feng shui is practiced.

FLYING STAR CHART OF A PERIOD 8 HOUSE FACING SW1

SE	S	SW
3 6 7 1 5 8		
7 **3** **5**		
E 4 7 2 5 9 3 W		
6 **8** **1**		
8 2 6 9 1 4		
2 **4** **9**		
NE	N	NW

Shown above is a typical flying star chart. Looking at it, take note of the compass directions indicated for each little square. This is how you will be superimposing the numbers onto the different sectors of your house. Remember that Flying Star is a compass formula, so you will need a good compass.

Period Number

The largest number of each little grid is referred to as the period number from which the other two little numbers are derived. By simply looking at the large number in the center of the square, you will know that the chart is of a Period 8 house. If the center period number is 7, then it is a period 7 house. In this chart, the center number is 8, so this is a period 8 house.

The period number reveals the general luck of each of the compass sectors of the home. Generally, the numbers 1, 6 and 8 are excellent numbers that connote good things and good fortune. The numbers 5 and 2 bring loss and illness. The number 3 brings quarrels and misunderstandings. The number 4 brings love and romance. The number 7 brings burglary luck, while the number 9 is a magnifying number. These meanings of the numbers apply irrespective of whether you are looking at the big or the small numbers.

Water Star & Mountain Star Numbers

Next take note of the water star numbers and the mountain star numbers. Every little square has a water star and a mountain star, and the numbers will tell you which of the compass sectors of your home has good water star luck and which has bad water star luck. The same applies for the mountain star. The water star is the little number on the right hand side of the big number, while the mountain star is the little number on the left hand side.

These two stars are actually more important, and their influence on the feng shui of the house is more powerful than that indicated by the period numbers. The water star governs everything to do with income luck and accumulations of wealth, while the mountain star has to do with luck in all your relationships. It also governs your health luck.

Thus when you look at a flying star chart of your house, you are actually holding in your hand a map of the *luck distribution* of your house. Knowing this luck distribution opens up the practice of Flying Star feng shui to you, because now you will be able to design the layout of your home in a way that maximizes the luck potential of your house.

You will also be able to design the flow of chi in your home so that energy moves in a harmonious fashion bringing a sense of balance and settled stability to residents. Most importantly, you will know how to activate the good numbers thereby ensuring that success luck is obtained to bring you satisfaction in all your endeavours; and you will know how to guard yourself against bad luck by suppressing and controlling the indicated bad luck numbers. For a complete set of Period 8 charts go to Tip 104 on page 218.

92

THE STARS IN THE CHART ARE NUMBERS

ow that you have familiarized yourself with a typical flying star chart and can see what it looks like, you are ready to learn how to construct a flying star chart. Note that the "stars" referred to are not real stars. They are actually numbers, with each number representing and signifying different attributes and meanings. Remember that in each of the nine grids there is a period star numeral, a mountain star numeral and a water star numeral. Look at the chart here of a Period 7 house. This is a house that faces South.

The star numerals are different in each grid. If you examine the flying star chart shown here, you can see that it shows a period of 7 house (because the main numeral in the center is 7). We also know that this house is facing South and there is a main door located here in the South sector of the house.

The center water star is the number 2 and this is the period number of the South sector where the house facing direction is. This South sector is known as the <u>facing palace</u> and the number here becomes the water star in the center grid.

So from the example given here, the *water star* in the center grid is number 2, so this tells us the house is facing South. Why? This is because the water star in the center of the chart is always the main numeral of the facing palace. Thus note that the main number of the South grid is 2, so the water star in the center of the chart is 2. Once we have the center number of the water star we can fill in the water star numbers of the other grids that make up the natal chart. This is done following the same sequence of numbers of the period numbers.

Next, note that the mountain star in the center grid is 3. This tells me the house is sitting North (because the main number in the North is 3). Once again, note that according to the formula, the mountain star in the center is the main numeral of the sitting palace. And once we have the center number of the mountain star, it is possible to fill in the rest of the mountain star numbers around the chart.

In Flying Star, you must always look at the water stars and mountain stars. These exert a far bigger influence on your feng shui than the period stars. The water stars govern your financial luck, while the mountain stars govern your relationship and health luck.

93

CHARTING THE NUMBERS

How do we fill in the rest of the water star and mountain star numbers in the flying star chart? How do we chart the numbers? We do this by determining the flight path of the numbers as they move around the chart. First we need to know the path itself. Here we need to go back to the original Lo Shu square to carefully take note of the way the numbers move from the center to the NW to the West, to the NE, to the South, to the North, to the SW, to the East and finally to the SE. This is shown in the Lo Shu square. The other illustration showing the arrows formed by the flight path of the numbers emphasizes this flight path.

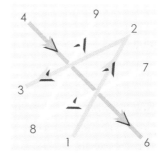

LO SHU SQUARE   **FLIGHT PATH OF NUMBERS**

Next we need to determine if the center numbers of the water and mountain stars are plus or minus. Whether it is plus or minus depends on whether the center numbers are odd or even. It also depends on the facing direction of the house.

The plus or minus of the center number of the water and mountain stars is based on the following table here which shows that when the facing direction is the first subdirection i.e. South 1, then even numbers are minus while odd numbers are plus. When the house is facing the second and third subdirections South 2 or South 3, then even numbers are plus and odd numbers are minus.

	Sub Direction		
Facing Direction	1	2	3
Odd	+	-	-
Even	-	+	+

This reference table will help you remember when the water and mountain stars fly plus or minus.

Flying plus means the stars move from grid to grid in a positive ascending order i.e. from 3 to 4 to 5. Note that the mountain or water star in the center can fly plus or minus from grid to grid. When flying plus, the number ascends as it moves from the center to the NW, to the West, to the NE, to the South, to the North, to the SW, to the East and finally to the SE. This path from one direction to the next is referred to as the *flight path* of the numbers.

Flying minus means the stars are moving from grid to grid in a negative descending order i.e. from 2 to 1, to 9 and so on. When the water star in the center is flying minus, the number descends as it moves from the center to the NW, to the West, to the NE, to the South, to the North, to the SW, to the East and finally to the SE. This path from one direction to the next is referred to as the *flight path* of the numbers.

Flying Star feng shui examines all the numerals in all the nine grids and draw conclusions about the luck of the sectors of a dwelling place during a specific time period. All this analysis is based on the numbers that come together in each sector. The nine grids are known as the *nine palaces*.

94

DETERMINING THE PERIOD

The numbers to be used in the analysis must be charted correctly. When the computation of the star numerals is not done correctly, the analysis is sure to be flawed to the extent that serious mistakes can result. To ensure accuracy of the practice, you need to get the correct period of your house i.e. when it was built or renovated. So you need to **determine the period** when your house was built OR when it was last renovated.

Thus if your house was built in 1946, that makes it a period 5 house and the starting point is a Lo Shu square with the main numeral 5 in the center. However, if the house was extensively renovated say in 1985, this renovation will transform it into a Period 7 house, and then the main numeral in the center will be the one with the number 7. Determining the period of the house gives you the base chart of numbers with the entire period numbers set out in the nine palaces.

Now exactly what constitutes a renovation, or how a house changes period is a fairly controversial issue amongst feng shui masters. It seems that there are differences of opinion that present significant consequences on the chart that is to be used for analysis. Because this is quite a controversial issue, it is necessary to think through this matter so that readers can decide for themselves which approach seems to be the most reasonable.

95 BASE CHARTS OF DIFFERENT PERIODS

SE	S	SW
4	9	2
E 3	5	7 W
8	1	6
NE	N	NW

A PERIOD OF 5 BASE CHART

This is also the original Lo Shu Square. If your house was built between the years 1944 and 1964, or if this was the time when it was last renovated, then to chart your flying star numbers, you should use this Lo Shu square with this sequence of main numerals in the various sectors to get started. If however your house was renovated after Feb 4th 1964 you will have to move on to a different Lo Shu square, one with a 6 in the center, as this is what reflects the correct period of your house.

Note that old houses of a previous period have what is known as very "tired energy". The chi is weak and luck is usually limited. When you renovate your house you are revitalizing it. This is a very essential part of practicing feng shui. All houses change energies from period to period and have to be re energized. When periods change, houses must be renovated to follow the change, otherwise residents' luck instantly gets weakened. Note that the world has just changed from period 7 to period 8 and this occurred on February 4th 2004. As such, all of you currently living in houses built or renovated before that date should seriously consider renovating to bring your house into line with the new period's energy. Even if you live in an apartment, you should consider changing the energy with a renovation. This is one of the most important things to undertake if you want to ensure that you continue to enjoy good fortune.

A PERIOD OF 6 BASE CHART

Note the number 6 in the center of the square. Because the number in the center has changed, all the other numbers also change. It is useful for you to see how the numbers change because this charts the flight of the numbers.. i.e. how 5 becomes 6, and 6 becomes 7 and 7 becomes 8 and so forth. Once you familiarize yourself with the "flight" of the numbers, you will start to discern the pattern of the movement. So far we are seeing the numbers move in an ascending order and this is known as flying in a yang or plus mode. Numbers can also fly in a yin or minus mode when it comes to the mountain and water stars. This is denoted by the plus or minus sign against the water and mountain stars.

A PERIOD OF 7 BASE CHART

The number in the center has become 7 and again as a result of this, all the numbers in the other grids of the square has also changed. This is the Lo Shu to use for all houses or buildings built or renovated between Feb 4th 1984 and Feb 4th 2004. This is the Lo Shu of Period 7, the previous period. Because the period has changed, the number 7 which used to be so lucky prior to February 4th 2004 has now become unlucky. Later on, when we come to the interpretation of numbers, you will see that the number that signifies the current period is considered exceptionally lucky, while the number that represents the immediately past period is considered very weak, and it also reverts to its original nature.

SE	S	SW
7	3	5
E 6	8	1 W
2	4	9
NE	N	NW

A PERIOD OF 8 BASE CHART

This is the base chart of the current period of 8. Once again you will notice that the numbers of all the other sectors have also changed. This is the base placement of numbers used to chart the numbers for all houses built or renovated after Feb 4th 2004 until Feb 4th 2024. Since we are currently in the Period of 8, the number 8 has become exceptionally lucky. It also signifies that we have entered an Earth period, because 8 is an earth number which also stands for the mountain. Hence while Period 7 was a time for making money Period 8 is a time for looking after our health, longevity and relationships. Period 8 is also a time when natural disasters and violence, bloodshed and war becomes a serious issue. This is because the number 7 has reverted to its original nature and has become a force for evil. For twenty years, the number 7 brought good luck, but now, the number 7 brings disasters, burglary, voilence and bloodshed. It is definitely very important to change your house into a Period 8 home if you want to suppress the bad energies of 7, especially if yours is a Period 7 house.

96   WHAT CONSTITUTES A RENOVATION

When deciding which Lo Shu square is the correct one to use for your house, you might be fazed by the term "renovation". Not all feng shui masters agree on what constitutes a renovation. Some experts say the renovation has to be very extensive, others maintain that all you need to do is close the home for three months and then reopen it to constitute a renovation and thus a change of period. Those of you currently changing your homes into Period 8 homes will be confronting this dilemma.

Certain Flying Star experts have indicated to me that only a major renovation that involves the addition of new floor space accompanied by the changing of the entire roof with a lot of banging and building qualifies as a renovation for purposes of changing the period of one's house for Flying Star analysis. This is the kind of renovation that is strong enough to change the flying star period and hence the Lo Shu square center numeral.

Other masters insist that a repainting and change in soft furnishings is sufficient to count as a renovation.

Personally, I believe this is a matter of judgment. For me, I do not consider a repaint and interior décor job a renovation that is sufficient to change the period of your house. But I do not think one has to change the entire roofline for there to be a change of period. As long as there is banging, drilling, tearing down of walls and rebuilding of some parts of the house including some parts of the floor and roof, this should count as renovation strong enough to change the period. Thus if you have done something like this to your house anytime from Feb 4th 2004 to the present, then irrespective of when your house was built, yours will qualify as a Period 8 house, and the main star numeral in the center will be 8. *This will be your starting point.*

A recent development in this issue has arisen since the last time I wrote about Flying Star. It seems that a famous feng shui master has now decided that one does not even need to renovate a house to change its period. All that is needed according to this practitioner is that the house be left empty for one hundred days for it to change its period! This interpretation, if correct, is good news for apartment dwellers that have little or no control over the period change of the whole apartment building that houses their apartment.

Now, according to the new interpretation, to change the period of their apartment (and this is becoming crucial since we have just moved into the new Period of 8), all they need to do is move out of their apartment for 100 days, and then move back in again. Leaving the apartment empty will cause its energy to wilt. Then moving in again introduces new energy! This is how the energy of the apartment gets changed. This is of course a very convenient way to rationalize.

Another mainstream feng shui practitioner has also suggested that if you are unable to change your period, then creating a window or door in the Northwest is sufficient for the period 8 energy to enter into the home!

Basically I prefer to play safe and undertake real and serious renovations (which I have done) to change my Period 7 house into a Period 8 house. But like I said, this is a matter of judgement.

97 THE FACING DIRECTION

There is also controversy surrounding step two in the charting of flying star numbers and this has to do with determining the facing direction of the house. The facing direction is crucial because it determines the center numeral of the water and mountain stars, which in fact are the crucial numbers to analyze in any flying star chart.

Generally, the facing direction of the house is the same as the facing direction of its main door – this is in fact the way it should be if one is to enjoy positively good feng shui. In the old days when feng shui was used in ancient China, this was almost always the case. BUT in today's age when modern day and contemporary houses, especially bungalows and mansions, come in such a huge variety of styles – from modular to sprawling to irregular shapes – a simple matter of determining the facing direction of the houses has become something of a challenge.

Most Flying Star masters are now agreed that it is the house facing direction rather than the facing direction of the main door that determines the flying star chart.

So note that the facing direction of the house:

a. need not be the same as the facing direction of the main door
b. is usually the direction in front of which is empty space or busy yang energy
c. does not need to be the same as where the main door is located
d. for apartments is the facing direction of the whole building

e.   can sometimes be the direction where there is a large balcony or picture window

Onsite investigation is important in determining the facing direction of difficult cases and you will have to use your visual judgement. There are houses that come in irregular shapes, that are modular in concept, and which may have several different wings. In such instances, experience does help, but more than experience is the logic behind the whole investigation. At some point, however, decisions do have to be made, and I have to say that I have come across buildings which are simply impossible to analyze with flying star charts.

For example in the case of houses or apartment buildings that have no clear cut facing direction, or which have so many entrances that one gets instantly confused. In such cases, my experience has been that the chi also gets confused, and luck is at best, erratic. When you are really stumped, my advice is to use two different facing directions to chart the numbers and then through analysis of the history of residents, you can determine which is the most likely chart that applies to the home.

TIPS ON TAKING DIRECTIONS

You should take the direction three times on a compass you are familiar with. Stand just inside the house, or at the doorway of the house, then three feet inside and next perhaps three feet outside. You will have to find a convenient place to determine this facing direction accurately.

The three directions taken could be different and this is quite normal.

Small variances are to be expected since compass readings are affected by magnetic energy caused by the presence of metal in the structural pillars as well as in metallic objects nearby. Sometimes the steel contained within walls cause so much havoc to some compasses that quite a wide margin of direction change occurs. Seismic ground activity has the same effect. So it is a good idea to find a place to measure the direction without it being too affected by metallic disturbances. When in doubt, remember that it is where the chi enters your home that is most significant, so one reading should always be near the vicinity of the main door.

Also make certain that your compass is held level to the ground around waist level. Some compasses come with a water leveler and this always helps. The direction you are measuring should also be 'square' to the houses. This means you must ensure that the angle of reading is correct, so pressing the compass to the wall sometimes helps.

Once you are set to take directions, use the compass to determine which of the 8 directions and which of the 24 mountains of the Earth Plate best measures the <u>house facing direction</u>.

For example the house may be facing EAST, but you need to take note which of the three subdirections of East it faces i.e. East 1, East 2 or East 3. Both pieces of information are required to chart the numbers because, as we have seen earlier, while it is the facing direction that determines the number of the water star number in the center, it is the subdirection it faces that determines whether the water star numbers move from grid to grid in a plus (i.e. ascending) or minus (i.e. descending) order.

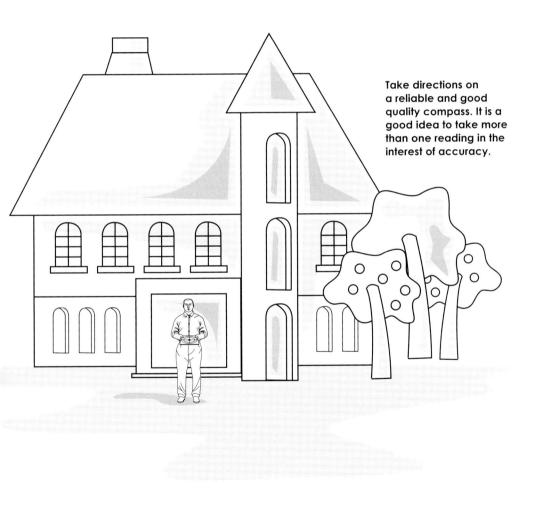

Take directions on a reliable and good quality compass. It is a good idea to take more than one reading in the interest of accuracy.

S tep three is to determine the water and mountain star numbers. Start by determining the center number of the water star (also known as the *siang sin*) and the mountain star (also known as the *chor sin*). The center number of the water star is the number of the facing direction of the house. The center mountain star number is the number of the house sitting direction. This is always the number opposite the facing direction.

So when the facing direction of the house is East, its sitting direction is West. When the facing direction is North the sitting direction is South. To obtain the numbers that represent the direction, we look at the PERIOD chart of the house. So if it is a Period 7 house, we look at a period 7 chart.

Below is the flying star chart of a Period 7 house, facing East. Let me walk you through how the water and mountain stars are placed in the center.

PERIOD 7 HOUSE FACING EAST 1

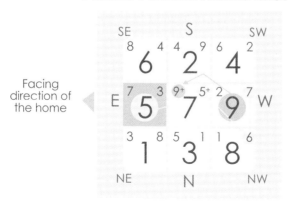

The center water star 5 is from the main numeral of the facing palace (East). The center mountain star 9 is from the main numeral of the sitting palace (West).

PERIOD 7 HOUSE FACING EAST in sub-direction E1

i) Note the main number of the EAST grid is 5.

ii) This becomes the number of the center water star.

iii) Since 5 is an odd number the flight path for the water stars around the whole chart flies *plus, minus, minus*. This means it flies plus when the house facing direction is E1, and it flies minus when the house facing direction is E2 or E3. In this case, since the house is facing E1, the water stars fly plus i.e. the numbers fly an ascending order.

iv) Next we look at number opposite East 5 to determine the center mountain star. This is the main number in the West where the number is 9. This is the sitting direction number and it becomes the mountain star number in the center. Since the number of the mountain star is odd, its flight path is exactly the same as that of the water star. So the next mountain star from the center which is in the NW is the number 1, ascending from 9. In the next grid West, the mountain star is 2 and so on.

See if you can work out the number of the mountain stars in the other palaces of the whole chart. Remember to move in the same sequence as the water stars moved. In this example, the numbers are changing in an ascending manner from grid to grid because the numbers are moving in a plus mode.

The result of placing all the water stars and mountain stars on the right and left of the main star numerals completes the flying star chart. By analyzing this chart, a great deal of extremely useful information about the luck of this house that is facing East 1 and was built in the Period of 7 can be revealed.

In this book, all the Period 7 and 8 flying star charts have been cast for easy reference. So if you are having a hard time learning how to cast the flying star chart, you can skip this section and move straight to the analysis sections. For those determined to master the method, let us move on to another example.

100   ANOTHER WORKED EXAMPLE

H ere is another example to show how the water stars and mountains stars of a flying star chart are determined. In this example, we are looking at a Period 7 house that is facing Northwest in subsection NW 1. See if you can follow the logic behind the numbers shown in the chart.

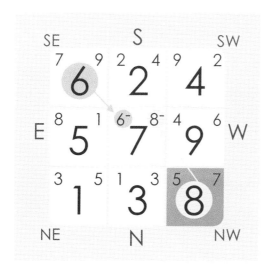

This Period 7 house is facing Northwest. Note that the main number of the NW is 8, so this number becomes the center number of the water star. Because this number is an even number, the water star numbers will fly Minus, Plus, Plus. In this case, since the door faces NW1, the water stars fly MINUS, i.e. in a descending fashion. So the water star becomes 7 in the NW and 6 in the West, 5 in the NE and so on.

209

Meanwhile, for the mountain stars, we look at the sitting direction main number. The sitting direction is opposite NW, which is SE, and here the main number is 6. This becomes the mountain star number in the center. Because 6 is an even number, it flies *Minus, Plus, Plus*. Since this house is facing the first subdirection i.e. NW 1, the stars will fly in a *minus* fashion i.e. in a descending order. So the center mountain star of 6 becomes 5 in the NW, and 4 in the West, 3 in the NE and so on.

Note that both water and mountain stars fly in the same sequential arrangement as the main star numerals, which is the flight path of the numbers.

You can use the same method for computing Period 8 Flying Star charts. However you should know that since 8 is an Earth period, the way the water stars and mountain stars "fly" in all houses facing Earth directions SW or NE will be the opposite of the conventional way. Thus here odd numbers fly minus, plus, plus, and even numbers fly plus, minus, minus.

101 USEFUL TIPS IN CHARTING NUMBERS

Here are some useful tips to remember

- Note that when we look at period charts, the numbers in the nine palaces are no longer in their original Lo Shu arrangement. The numbers in the nine palaces have "moved" – and so the 3 numbers in a row no longer add up to 15. You will be surprised how many people still get confused by this.

- Remember the movement of the numbers from the center outwards does not move in a haphazard manner. Every one of the "stars" or numbers from 1 to 9 always move around the nine palaces in a set pattern. This follows the placement of numbers in the original Lo Shu Square with the numeral 5 in the center. Every feng shui practitioner who wants to practice Flying Star feng shui must commit this flight pattern to memory. To practice, all you need to do is look at the way the numbers change from one palace to the next.

- Remember the flight of the water and mountain stars can be ascending or descending – what we term plus or minus. To determine if the numbers fly plus or minus, just remember that ODD numbers fly plus, minus minus for 1st, 2nd and 3rd subdirection, while EVEN numbers fly minus, plus, plus for the 1st, 2nd, and 3rd directions.

-     Now this rule is true for Period 7 charts. But in the Period of 8 (and in some other period charts) there is an exception to this rule. Note that Period 8 houses that face SW or NE do not follow the conventional plus minus minus rule. Since the Period 8 charts will also be given in their entirety, you need only take note of this exception to the rule in case you get confused should you attempt to "fly the stars" when charting the numbers for Period 8 houses. All you need to do really is to use your compass to determine the facing direction of your house, determine the period of your house and then refer to all the different charts. Then select the chart that applies to your house based on you house facing direction and its period.

SUMMARY OF STEPS FOR CHARTING FLYING STAR NUMBERS

1. Determine the period of the house or building to establish the base chart.

2. Determine the facing direction of the house, property or building.

3. Determine the subdirection of the facing direction.

4. Determine the center number of the water and mountain stars.

5. Determine if the center numbers of the water and mountain stars are odd or even.

6. Determine if the water and mountain stars are flying plus or minus.

7. Determine the water star numbers in the nine palaces by "flying" the water star numbers.

8. Determine the mountain stars in the nine palaces by "flying" the mountain star numbers.

9. When you have charted the flying star numbers of your house, superimpose them onto your house layout plan for analysis.

102 MOUNTAIN & WATER STARS

M any expert practitioners of Flying Star focus only on the combination of the water star numbers and mountain star numbers in each of the nine palaces, and especially in the "palace" where the main door, master bedroom are located. And indeed these are the two sets of numbers that reveal most of the vital information relating to the wealth, health and happiness luck of residents.

Summarized here are the basic attributes of the water and mountain stars, which are useful to bear in mind when we go deeper into flying star numbers analysis in the next section.

THE WATER STAR (also known as the *siang sin* star).

The siang sin star symbolizes wealth and prosperity prospects. It signifies career luck, financial status, wealth accumulation, growth and business prospects of the residents. Known as the water star, it is symbolic of riches. Having an auspicious water star in the sector where your front door, office or study, or master bedroom is located brings you the luck of wealth and prosperity.

Thus if the main door is located where the number 8 siang sin star is found during this current period of 8, it is a very auspicious sign for the residents of the household. The water star 8 is regarded as very auspicious, and wealth luck will be hugely magnified if you are able to "activate" it with the presence of water.

If your main door is located in a sector where the water star 8 is present, and if the door is facing an open area, this is extremely lucky because chi can then settle and accumulate while being energized by the water star 8. The chi improves further with the presence of physical water, and residents will become extremely wealthy during the Period of 8. Luck is further improved when the water is correctly built according to feng shui requirements to energize water features. For instance when there is a fishpond there, it signifies abundance. When there is a spring there, it signifies water bubbling up from the ground bringing wealth from the earth. And when there are flows of water feeding the pond, it signifies many sources of income.

In apartments, the possibilities are not as extensive as when you have a landed property with garden. Nevertheless you can place an aquarium or six-tier waterfall in the corner of the living and dining room that corresponds to the auspicious water star 8 sector of the flying star chart of the house. Knowing where the auspicious water star number 8 is located in your house is a very valuable piece of information. Many people bring the feng shui consultant into the house or office just to accurately determine this. Activating the water star 8 is the best way of attracting wealth luck into the house. The key lies in correctly identifying the part of the house that has the luckiest water star, which is water star 8. However, the water star 6 and water star 1 are also considered to be very lucky.

THE MOUNTAIN STAR (also known as the *chor sin* star)
The *chor sin* star governs the health prospects of the house, as well as relationship luck, romance, love, family authority and mental attitudes. Like the water star, the mountain star is also most auspicious when the numeral is 8, so determining where the mountain star 8 is located in your house is the key to unlocking excellent health and relationship luck.

The number assigned to each of the *chor sin* stars in the different palaces indicates the quality of the resident's health, social standing and popularity. When the mountain star number is 8 and it occurs in the palace where the main door, bedroom or any important room is located, it brings excellent good fortune.

When the numbers are afflicted, then health takes a turn for the worse. Afflicted mountain stars are those with the numbers 5 or 2. These numbers indicate sickness and severe ill health that can be fatal, especially when the same numbers 5 and 2 also occur in the same corner during any month or year.

An auspicious mountain star is the one that corresponds to the number of the current period. Thus in the period of 8, the mountain star 8 is auspicious. There are also other auspicious numbers associated with the mountain star, most important of which are the numbers 6 and 1.

HOW THE NUMBERS COMBINE

Flying Star number analysis goes beyond merely looking at the mountain and water stars in isolation. What is important is to see the way the numbers combine. There are three sets of number combinations that are important when analyzing flying star charts. These are:

1. Water and mountain star combinations
2. Water and main star combinations
3. Mountain and main star combinations

In undertaking any analysis, we should take note of:
1. The meanings of individual numbers.
2. The meanings of number combinations.
3. The meanings of element interactions of the numbers.
4. The effect of incoming element on the element of the palace.
5. The strength of the numbers in the current period.
6. Meanings of special combinations.

For residents to feel the full impact of the star numbers, be they good or bad, the numbers have to be activated. Water stars are activated by activity, by the presence of water, holes, lower land, and by the presence of certain symbols. When the water star number is an unlucky number, activating it causes loss of wealth and when the star number is auspicious, activating it brings wealth luck. The numbers that the water star combines with gives further clues to the nature and essence of its good or bad luck.

Mountain stars are activated by stillness and quiet, by the presence of "mountains", crystals, walls, statues, sculptures and ceramic symbols of good fortune.

Once again, when the mountain star numbers are unlucky, activating with stones, boulders or higher land causes severe illness to manifest, while activating auspicious mountain star numbers bring fame, recognition, victory, authority, power or popularity.

Mountain stars always affect the luck that deals with one's relationships and this covers all kinds of relationships. When you live in a room afflicted by bad mountains stars, it is unlikely that your relationships with people in general will be pleasant. On the other hand, when the mountain star in your room is lucky, then you enjoy the good fortune of having relationships that bring you a great deal of happiness and good fortune.

104 PERIOD 7 FLYING STAR CHARTS

I f your house or building was built or renovated between Feb 4th 1984 and Feb 4th 2004, it is a Period 7 house and one of these sixteen charts presented here will apply to your house or building. To determine which chart applies to your house, use a compass to determine the facing direction of your house. In most cases, this is the same as the facing direction of your main door. However, this is not always the case, so you will need to take a good look at your house, then determine which is its correct facing direction.

Please note that Flying Star feng shui divides the compass directions into 24 directions. Each of the main directions has three subdirections so it is necessary to see which of the 24 directions your house facing direction belongs to. Note that the second and third subdirections have the same flying star chart. Thus there are 16 charts for each period.

Feng shui practitioners may use these charts to undertake detailed analysis of Period 7 houses and buildings. Those whose homes or buildings are of a previous earlier period will need to construct the flying star chart applicable to their period.

PERIOD 7 FLYING STAR CHARTS

Facing South 1

Facing S2 or S3

Facing East 1

Facing E2 or E3

Facing SW1

Facing SW2 or SW3

Facing SE1

Facing SE2 or SE3

PERIOD 7 FLYING STAR CHARTS

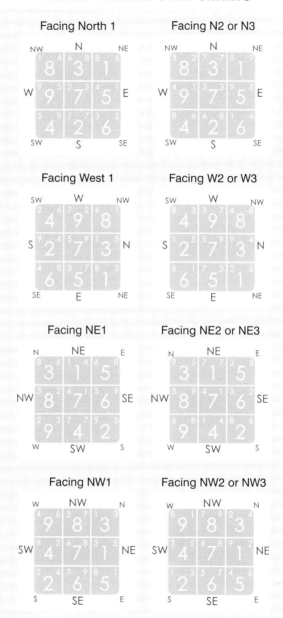

Facing North 1

8	3	1
9	7	5
4	2	6

Facing N2 or N3

8	3	1
9	7	5
4	2	6

Facing West 1

4	9	8
2	7	3
6	5	1

Facing W2 or W3

4	9	8
2	7	3
6	5	1

Facing NE1

3	1	5
8	7	6
9	4	2

Facing NE2 or NE3

3	1	5
8	7	6
9	4	2

Facing NW1

9	8	3
4	7	1
2	6	5

Facing NW2 or NW3

9	8	3
4	7	1
2	6	5

105 PERIOD 8 FLYING STAR CHARTS

I f your house or building was recently built or renovated after Feb 4th 2004 (and until Feb 4th 2024) then your house or building is no longer a Period 7 house. Instead, it has become a Period 8 house, in which case one of these sixteen charts presented overleaf applies to your house or building.

To determine the chart that applies to your house, first determine the compass facing direction of your house or building. Please note that Flying Star feng shui divides each of the compass main directions into three subdirections of fifteen degrees each. Note also that the second and third subdirections share the same flying star chart. There are thus 16 charts from which to select the correct chart for your house.

PERIOD 8 FLYING STAR CHARTS

PERIOD 8 FLYING STAR CHARTS

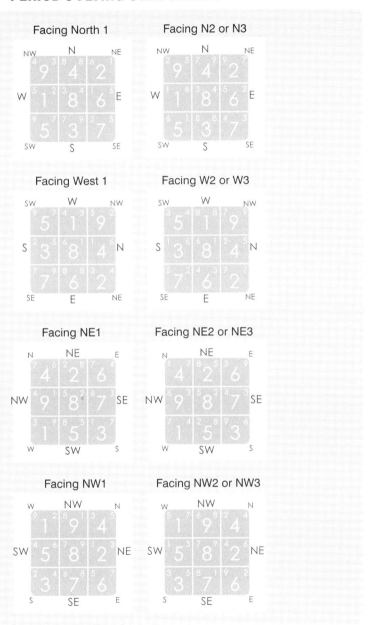

Facing North 1

Facing N2 or N3

Facing West 1

Facing W2 or W3

Facing NE1

Facing NE2 or NE3

Facing NW1

Facing NW2 or NW3

DIFFERENTIATE THE FIVE TYPES OF STARS

The flying star chart of any building has five types of "stars" and these are expressed as numbers between 1 and 9. This method of feng shui is sometimes described as the study of Chinese numerology because it requires the interpretation of numbers and combinations of numbers that are charted and placed inside a nine-by-nine grid based on the famous Chinese magic square known as the Lo Shu square. The chart with the numbers inside each of the grids reveals information that tells the practitioner what adjustments are needed to improve the feng shui of the house. Flying Star charts reveal information on different aspects of luck for residents of the household.

Before you analyse numbers and number combinations to determine their lucky or unlucky implications, first examine what kind of stars you are analyzing. It is necessary to differentiate between the Period Star, Water star, Mountain Star, Annual Star and Monthly Star. These are five kinds of stars have a direct influence over the feng shui of your house from period to period, year to year and month to month.

THE PERIOD STAR

When analysis of a flying star chart is attempted, we first look at the Period Star, before moving on to the other stars. However, in terms of potency, the Period number in the chart is the least potent and its importance is due to it being the key that unlocks the placement of the mountain and water stars. So when it comes to interpretation of the chart, the Period Star number (usually depicted as the largest number in the chart) exerts the least influence.

THE WATER STAR

This star exerts the greatest influence and the number of the water star dominates the chi energy of the palace it occupies, often overcoming the effect of the Period and Mountain Stars. So it is necessary to study the Water Star number and whether it is good or bad, because it has the greatest strength in terms of its effect on residents. The water star rules the material well being of residents.

THE MOUNTAIN STAR

In terms of influence, the Mountain Star is more important than the Period Star but less strong than the Water Star in terms of influence. The number of the Mountain Star overrides the Period Star, but holds its own with the Water Star. The Mountain Star influences the health and relationship luck of residents.

ANNUAL AND MONTHLY STARS

The nature of feng shui is never static; so alongside the 20 year charts, the luck of houses does not stay the same all through those twenty years. This is where the annual and monthly charts come in. The numbers of the annual and monthly charts exert heavy influence over flying star chart numbers. annual and monthly stars exert an equally strong influence and usually when something goes very wrong, it is always a good idea to first check the annual and monthly star numbers in the important sectors of the house. Always take note of annual and monthly star numbers. This gives a comprehensive reading of chi distribution and luck of any home on a monthly basis.

107 PERIOD 8 HOUSES?

Period 8 houses have charts that contain some particular characteristics, which, when correctly activated have the potential to bring excellent wealth and relationship luck. Unlike houses of the immediately preceding period 7, four of the period 8 houses enjoy what are termed the "specials", which are combinations of numerals that indicate potent auspicious energy. These are charts where the numbers come together in extraordinary combinations that bring exceptional luck to residents.

Period 8 charts are characterized by the strategic placement of water and mountain stars that carry the numeral 8 – which are located in either the facing or the sitting palaces. This means feng shui water and mountain features should ideally be placed in front of or at the back of the house rather than by the sides. Correctly planning the design of your period 8 house therefore holds out the promise of extreme good fortune.

Houses that are renovated or completed anytime from now until Feb 4th 2024 are Period 8 houses. Such houses benefit from the energy of the current period and residents living in such houses generally enjoy much better feng shui luck than those living in houses of the preceding period of 7. The energy levels of their homes will be far more robust and vigorous.

Those still living in period 7 houses would benefit very much from converting their homes into period 8 homes. What they need to do is undertake a renovation of their home which should include changing at least a third of the roof and floor (which revitalizes heaven and earth energy) as well as changing the main door.

BEWARE THE DOUBLE 7

Period 7 houses that face Southwest, Northeast, South and North have the double 7 in either their facing or sitting palaces and while this brought good fortune for residents of such houses during the period from 1984 to 2004, in the current period, the double 7 brings only failure, setbacks and disappointments. Those who are unfortunate could also get robbed or become victims of violence. So period 7 houses facing these directions have an urgency to transform into period 8.

FOCUS ON THE CENTER GRIDS

Those renovating their homes into Period 8 houses or designing their new homes, please take note that they must not waste the center grid of their houses on staircases, toilets or store rooms.

I am referring to the center of the width of the house and this would include the facing and sitting palaces. This is because an essential characteristic of Period 8 charts is that the auspicious water star 8 and mountain star 8 are located in either the facing or sitting palaces.

So if your house is too narrow or is only two rooms wide, you in effect "lose" the center grids. The house cannot then be anywhere near as lucky as it can be. So please protect your center grids.

108 WATER & MOUNTAIN IN PERIOD 8 HOUSES

THE DOUBLE 8

If you study all sixteen of the period 8 flying star charts, you will realize that all houses facing South, North, East and West (i.e. the primary directions of the compass) will have what is referred to as the double 8 in their charts. In these houses, both water and mountain stars 8 occur together in either the facing or sitting palaces depending on the subfacing direction of the house. Some feng shui experts are of the opinion that the double 8 attribute is more of a liability than a sign of good fortune, and this is based on their assumption that the residents of such houses can only benefit from either the water star 8 or the mountain star 8. They are of the opinion that residents cannot enjoy the benefits of both the water and mountain star 8 together.

According to flying star feng shui, when there is "water" or low land in the sector where an auspicious mountain star occurs, the mountain is described as "falling into the water", and this results in the good relationship and health luck being compromised. Hence, in activating the water star 8, the mountain star 8 could simultaneously get compromised.

However, I have discovered that the double 8 feature is something that can be turned to residents' advantage. The solution is to build a waterfall type of water feature in the facing palace (front of house) or in the sitting palace (back of house), wherever the double 8 occurs. This successfully taps both water and mountain thereby assuring residents of both wealth as well as relationship and health luck.

Just make sure that the accumulation of water is not larger than the "mountain" you build to accommodate the fall of water. But do let the pool be deep enough to make sure your wealth luck has depth!

A waterfall feature means a pool of water that is landscaped to incorporate a simulated mountain with water falling down it into a pond. This kind of water feature is the best way to activate the double 8 water and mountain stars. In doing this, you can also incorporate excellent tips from the water classics on feng shui and this means making certain the flow of water is coming towards an entrance into the home. There should be a door or window facing the waterfall to ensure the water and mountain energy can successfully "flow" into the home. Another suggestion is that the water should fall over six levels as this is considered to be exceptionally lucky. Having a dragon image near the water is also advisable and do not make the waterfall too imposing, as this might overwhelm the house.

WATER IN FRONT OF PERIOD 8 HOUSES

WATER STAR 8 IN FRONT

Houses facing the secondary directions of SW 1, NE 1, SE 2/3 and NW 2/3 will discover that they have the water star 8 in the facing palace (i.e. in the front of the house) and the mountain star 8 at the back of the house in the sitting palace. So in these houses waterfalls are not appropriate.

The situation here is excellent and many feng shui experts consider this to be an ideal situation. Indeed, many experts go to great lengths to ensure that the facing orientations conform to these directions, as having the water star 8 in front brings multiple feng shui benefits to the home, especially when a pool of water can be built to activate the water star 8. In so doing, the water simultaneously activates other benefits according to other formulas of feng shui.

For instance, according to landscape feng shui, it is truly ideal to have water in front of the house. When residents have their home facing water, it always brings excellent wealth luck.

Water at the front of the house also brings excellent "sheng chi" luck. This means "growth luck" as this part of the house is washed with growth energy that can only get activated by the presence of water. This is based on the Eight Mansions formula of feng shui.

Having water in front of the house in the location that conforms to the facing palace is deemed most beneficial. Having the water star 8 of the flying star chart here is therefore incredibly lucky.

MOUNTAIN AT THE BACK

MOUNTAIN STAR 8 BEHIND

With the prosperity luck of these secondary direction facing houses taken care of, we next turn our attention to the other vital component of good feng shui and this is the luck of relationships and good health brought by the mountain star 8. Implicit in the health luck is longevity luck and protection against premature death, so the mountain star 8 brings enormously important luck. Note that the number 8 itself also symbolizes the mountain, and we are in the period of the mountain, thus the mountain star has taken on great significance.

To activate the mountain star 8, the presence of a "physical mountain" or higher ground is necessary. This can be a high wall made of bricks and other earth element materials, or it can be a mound of boulders or simply higher ground. The best is to have a half moon shaped mountain at the back of the house as this is what also activates good landscape feng shui. This symbolizes the black tortoise which also gives the much needed support inherent in good landscape feng shui.

It is usually inappropriate to have lower ground at the back of the house unless there are "hills" or higher ground or tall buildings backing that. Even then, when there is lower ground behind the much needed mountain support is said to have fallen into the water, hence the house is no longer "protected". It is for this reason that having the mountain star 8 behind brings such good luck.

MOUNTAIN IN FRONT OF PERIOD 8 HOUSES

MOUNTAIN STAR 8 IN FRONT

Houses facing the secondary directions of SW 2/3, NE 2/3, SE 1 and NW 1 will discover that they have the MOUNTAIN star 8 in the facing palace (i.e. in the front of the house) and the water star 8 at the back of the house in the sitting palace. These houses face a difficult dilemma since activating their auspicious water and mountain stars 8 goes against the rules of landscape feng shui, which advises that water must be in front and mountain should be at the back.

With the mountain star 8 in front, there is a need to activate the front facing palace with a "mountain" which poses a threat as this could seriously block the luck of the residents. Mountains in front of the house almost always suggest obstacles to success. Yet it is necessary to activate the mountain star 8 here if the residents want to benefit from good relationship and health luck. Here are ways to deal with this kind of dilemma.

HOUSES FACING SW 2/3 & NW 2/3

Period 8 houses that face the second and third subsectors of the incredibly auspicious directions of SW and NE have nothing to worry about even if the mountain star 8 is in the facing palace. This is because both these houses enjoy what we term the parent string special combination — a very auspicious combination of numbers found in every one of the nine sectors of the home. The enormous good fortune of this "special" is explained later, but one of the side benefits of this is that it overrides any bad feng shui caused by having a "mountain" in front of the house. Indeed, in this instance, because of the situation of the reverse mountain reverse water in these two houses, there is a need to place mountain in front and water behind.

Thus in front it is acceptable to have a brick wall to signify a low mountain. This is sufficient to activate the mountain star 8 in front. It is however not advisable to have a pool or a fish pond. Instead, to activate for the benefits of having water here, it is a good idea to use a small water feature such as an aquarium or a small rotating ball sitting on top of overflowing water.

WATER STAR 8 BEHIND

As for the water star 8 at the back of the house, it is a good idea to install a small pond with water seeming to bubble up form the ground. This is an excellent way to activate the water star 8. At the same time, it is also beneficial to ensure there is simultaneously higher ground at the back to ensure adequate support for the residents.

In this case of the reverse water reverse mountain scenario of the flying star chart, residents can also build waterfall features in front and at the back of the house, thereby activating both water and mountain in front and at the back. The important thing to get right is to ensure that neither water nor mountain are so big as to overwhelm the house.

A waterfall successfully captures the "mountain" as well as the "water" - ideal for the reverse mountain reverse water situation.

The nine numbers in Flying Star are based on the observed traits of the nine "stars" that are the equivalent of the star formation of the great bear or the sickle which can be seen in the clear night sky. This is shown in the illustration here. The attributes of each of the numbers form the basis for the meaning of the numbers.

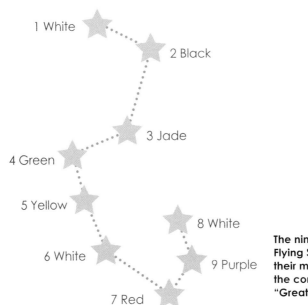

1 White

2 Black

3 Jade

4 Green

5 Yellow

8 White

6 White

9 Purple

The nine stars of the Flying Star chart take their meanings from the constellation of the "Great Bear".

7 Red

The three white numbers 1, 6 and 8 are the pure numbers that signify heaven's blessings. Of the three, 8 is deemed to have the greatest power to bring about a transformation from negative to positive as it has two assistants that dispense chastity and rewards. Hence the Chinese have always believed that 8 is the luckiest of the nine numbers. The number 8's right assistant is earth coloured representing the mountain star equivalent, while its left assistant is blue coloured representing the water star equivalent. Hence the number 8 is very efficient at bringing both wealth and relationship/health luck and irrespective of whether it occurs as mountain or water star, it brings amazing good fortune.

The two other white numbers 1 and 6 open doorways to wonderful opportunities.

The green number 4 brings literary accomplishments as well as romance. The number 4 is said to be a potentially seductive star which can also cause sexual misconduct. Its counterpart the number 3 is termed the jade star and signifies getting into trouble with the law. The number 3 has the potential for creating the cause for misunderstandings that can lead to aggravating court cases as well as very tragic consequences.

The number 7 is the broken soldier that represents injury and is often the result of violence and betrayal while greedy wolf, the number 2 black star brings sickness, illness and death. Here, note that the number 2 spells health concerns and the only time it stands for good health is during the Period of 2. In all other periods, the 2 star brings illness concerns.

Finally, the number 9, the last number signifies surplus harvest. This is a purple star that can also signify extreme good fortune. The number spells just before completion luck. It also has the ability to magnify good fortune or misfortune. It also suggests a time when it is auspicious to build for future prosperity.

113 THE LUCKY NUMBERS

The most auspicious numbers are the reigning number of the relevant period, which in the current period is the number 8. This means that from now until Feb 4th 2024, the number 8 is the luckiest number. 8 is also a white number and this makes it intrinsically lucky already. In addition, the other two white numbers are 1 and 6, so these are also very auspicious numbers. These are described as the white numbers 1, 6 and 8.

Here is a quick summary of their attributes during Period 8.

The number 1 signifies prosperity in the distant future

Because it represents water, and water means wealth or money, it is regarded favorably. It is also a white number and all white numbers are auspicious. The number 1 signifies the start of a new beginning. It symbolizes things getting better after having been bad. The number 1 as a water star number is especially auspicious because 1 stands for the element of water.

When it enters the East and Southeast, the number 1 manifests its "greedy wolf" persona. This is the name of 1 in the "Great Bear" or symbol of nine stars in the constellations. The number 1 has a positive persona as well as a negative side. When it shows its good side, the number 1 indicates success at a young age, fame and smart kids for the home. When the number 1 shows its bad side it can manifest as harm coming to the wife. This happens when it flies into the Southwest as a mountain star.

It can cause blindness when it clashes with the fire energy of the South. This means if it shows up as the mountain star in the South palace of the house, it can be dangerous. Sometimes such a configuration can lead to premature death. The number 1 has a strong effect on the fortunes of the middle son, and when it flies into the North, it brings either enhanced income to the son or it can bring marriage opportunities.

The number 6 represents faded prosperity that is now reviving

Because it is associated with the Trigram Chien, which means gold, it also stands for great power and influence. In fact, the number 6 is highly prized and every time it occurs in the NW sector, the patriarch of the home benefits and is said to be going through a good period then. The number 6 is generally regarded as the numeral that signifies heaven. It is also a white star, and in the Constellation of the "Great Bear", number 6 represents finance and everything to do with money. At its most positive, 6 represents power, influence, authority and great riches. At its most negative, the number 6 harms and exhausts the wife. In very bad instances where the 6 is severely afflicted it can cause death.

The number 8 during period eight reigns supreme

There is no number luckier than 8, and the number 8 is now entering its brightest period. This comes once in 180 years, so it is advisable to take fullest advantage of the current Period of 8, especially those with KUA number 8.

To activate the luck of this number, you should ensure that there is plenty of yang chi where 8 occurs in the chart. When there is movement, sound and activity, 8 brings plenty of good fortune. In the Constellation, 8 benefits the youngest son of the family, and at its most positive, 8 signifies great wealth, admirable honesty and nobility. At its most negative however, or when it gets afflicted either by harmful structures within the environment or by the presence of excessive metal energy, 8 can harm young children and cause sickness to manifest.

114 THE NUMBERS 1, 6, & 8

The white numbers 1, 6 and 8 bring varying degrees of good fortune wherever and whenever they occur either in flying star natal charts, in annual or monthly charts OR in the trigram charts. Of these three numbers, 8 is the most auspicious, while 6 brings the luck of heavens blessings. The number 1 brings victory and triumph over adversaries. Additional attributes of these numbers are related to their respective element and these are usually studied in the context of how their elements interact with the elements of the spaces they occupy in the charts and in different years.

Good fortune brought by the white star numbers apply in potent ways whether they appear as numbers in a flying star chart, or as numbers that fly into the different compass sectors in the annual chart of each year. They are equally potent in the monthly charts. The feng shui of Chinese numerology expressed in these numbers offer different applications. It is therefore beneficial to understand the meanings of these numbers thoroughly.

An important aspect of the numbers is the element represented by each of the numbers. In this context, the white numbers belong to the following elements.

The number 8 is an earth number
It is strengthened by fire energy, so when the number 8 occurs in the South direction, it becomes extra potent. Since we are now in the period of 8, this number has become a very powerful energizer of good fortune, so its appearance in your life as your phone number, your house number or as special numbers in your business will be very auspicious indeed. The number 8 also looks like the infinity sign which is recognized as a very powerful symbol in many cultures.

The number 8 also signifies the mountain, which is strong and unmovable. And remember, mountains contain many hidden treasures, but also many hidden dangers!

The number 6 belongs to the metal element

This number signifies the powerful trigram Chien, so it represents heaven and also stands for the patriarch. It suggests excellent mentor and leadership luck as well as obtaining strong support from influential people. The number 6 is strengthened by the element of earth so is especially beneficial when it occurs in the earth sectors of Southwest, Northeast and the center of any building or house. The number 6 brings unexpected and speculative luck.

The number 1 belongs to the water element

It is especially extra strong when it occurs in the North sector. This number works harmoniously when it flies into the metal sectors of West and Northwest, it then gets strengthened, but it does exhaust the energy of these sectors. It brings productive luck when it flies into the East and Southeast, and in these sectors it brings growth, manifesting abundance in often rather spectacular ways.

The powerful effect of these three numbers is felt most when they occur as either water stars or mountains stars in a flying star chart, and when activated with the physical presence of water or mountain, they have the potential to bring exceptional good fortune. Natural water such as lakes and mountains as well as lowlands and highlands are of course more beneficial, but man-made features will do just as well.

115 | NUMBER 1 BRINGS VICTORY & TRIUMPH

The number 1 star brings victory and triumph over competitors, so it is an especially good star number. The good fortune it attracts is usually related in some way to one's professional life; it affects career prospects and influences your luck at work or within a business environment. When you are in need of this kind of luck, search for the water star 1 and activate accordingly with water to increase your income luck at work, and then search for the mountain star 1 and activate with crystal or boulders. Both for the mountain star and the water star, the number 1 is regarded as a favourable number.

THE NUMBER 1 AS THE WATER STAR brings prosperity and success luck manifesting in excellent professional and career growth. This number is especially lucky when it occurs in your office at work or if you happen to sleep in a bedroom visited by the water star 1.

When the annual star 1 or monthly star 1 comes into the same grid, it usually causes good luck to manifest as career promotions and upward advancement. To activate the water star 1, place a bubbling water feature where it occurs. The water feature need not be large, but it needs to be yang and active. The water feature should not be placed in the bedroom since water in the bedroom can lead to loss and betrayal. The number 1 belongs to the water element and it is excellent when it flies into the North where the chi of the North harmonizes with it very well. It is also good when it flies into the wood sectors East and Southeast. It is not so good when it flies into the West and Northwest, as it tends to exhaust the energy of these two sectors. In the South it has the potential to clash with the element of fire there.

THE NUMBER 1 AS THE MOUNTAIN STAR brings good relationship luck in the work environment. It ensures harmony at work and opens up many opportunities in the career field through chance meetings and networking luck. If the mountain star in your office or bedroom is the number 1, you will have no difficulty obtaining the cooperation of colleagues and business associates. You only need to place a raw quartz crystal in your room to activate the mountain star 1, or if you wish, you can also place a boulder here to energize the earth element. Make sure the room is kept well lit and there are sounds and activity in the room. Then the good fortune described will have a better chance of manifesting.

The number 1 is water and it benefits wood sectors as water produces wood.

NUMBER 6 BRINGS HEAVEN'S BLESSINGS

The number 6 brings heaven's blessings. This is a number which had lost some chi energy during the Period of 7, but in the current Period of 8, it has become revitalized and has the strength to attract copious amounts of good fortune. It is usually associated with sudden and unexpected good fortune, the sort that comes without warning bringing lovely surprises.

THE NUMBER 6 AS THE WATER STAR brings divine luck that gets magnified when further supplemented by one's destiny luck. The number 6 stands for heaven and its equivalent trigram is that of CHIEN which signifies the leader or the patriarch. So the number 6 as the water star attracts good money luck for the leader, for the patriarch and for the head of the family.

In the period of 7, the number 6 lacked vitality and strength, but in the period of 8, this number has been revitalized and has the capability of attracting excellent good fortune. This is an especially lucky water star to activate with the presence of a water feature, especially with a six tier waterfall in the sector of the garden where it appears. If you opt to have this feature, the water should be placed outside the home in the appropriate corner where it occurs and the water feature that is built should best be a small waterfall with six levels of waterfall. The water must be seen to be entering the home so there should be a door or window to symbolically receive the water. This is the correct way of activating this excellent money-bringing water star.

If you place a water feature inside the house, do try to invest in one of those truly artistic Zen-type water features that keep water bubbling gently.

THE NUMBER 6 AS THE MOUNTAIN STAR brings lovely harmony luck and is excellent for spreading calm and happiness within the home. Wherever it occurs it is always a good idea to place six crystal or glass balls of varying sizes. This enhances the goodwill energy in the home making everyone very agreeable to each other and also ensuring that all social occasions proceed smoothly with little or no obstacles whatsoever.

The placement of six crystal balls is an understated yet most powerful feng shui feature that has many benefits. It is simply excellent to design this cluster of round spheres wherever you see the number 6 appearing as a mountain star. The crystal earth energy will also strengthen the metal element of the number - hence the elements are in harmony. The result is that everyone interacts harmoniously and agreeably. There will be minimum misunderstandings and little infighting.

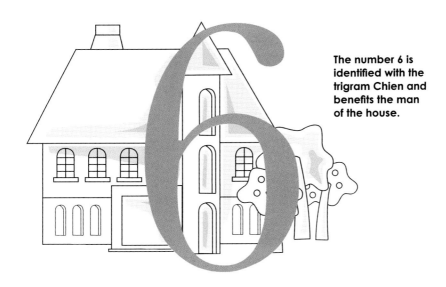

The number 6 is identified with the trigram Chien and benefits the man of the house.

117 NUMBER 8 BRINGS EXCELLENT LUCK

The number 8 is the luckiest number in this period and will stay lucky until Feb 4th 2024. It is the reigning number of the current period and in these next few years from 2008 onwards, the number is just "warming up to eventually reach its peak strength". This whole period is a time when wealth will arise from property ownership. This is due to the earth element of the number 8. The key to keeping the luck of 8 vigorous is to ensure plenty of fire element energy wherever it occurs. The number 8 enjoyed excellent chi energy during the period of 7, but in this period of 8 it has become even more powerful, enjoying what we term ripening luck.

THE NUMBER 8 AS THE WATER STAR brings abundant wealth luck, which gets magnified when it is properly activated by the presence of real water. This can be a pond or pool with some depth (at least 18 inches deep) and if possible, with a continuous flow of water coming into the pond to signify constant replenishment. The number 8 stands for the mountain and its equivalent trigram is that of KEN, which also signifies the youngest son. So this period tends to favour the young man.

When the number 8 is the water star, it attracts good money luck for everyone, but especially for the youngest son or only son of the family. In the period of 7, the number 8 was already very lucky; at that time, it signified future prosperity. Now that we are in the period of 8, the number signifies current prosperity, so for the current twenty years until Feb 4th 2024, the number 8 stands for good fortune that is ready to materialize.

However, if the water star 8 falls in your bedroom, you should not activate it with a water feature, as water in the bedroom creates loss. In the bedroom, it is unnecessary to activate the water star. Here, the energy of the couple is sufficient to energize the auspicious water star.

Having said that, do note that the best way to activate the water star 8 is still always a large water feature, preferably a pond that is dug into the ground. The act of digging is very auspicious for the corner BUT this should take place only in the garden or outdoors. You should refrain from digging inside the house UNLESS you are rebuilding the home. Never dig inside the home while you are still occupying it. This brings enormous bad luck!

THE NUMBER 8 AS THE MOUNTAIN STAR is excellent since the symbol of the number 8 is itself the mountain. Since the mountain star signifies good fortune in all your relationships, this means that when your room or office enjoys the presence of the mountain star 8, you will enjoy great popularity and have success in all your interactions with people. Your networking luck will be very successful and everyone will like you. If your bedroom enjoys the mountain star 8, it is truly very auspicious as it brings good health and harmonious relationships.

The best way to energize the mountain star 8 is with the symbolic presence of "mountains". Outside the house in the garden, this can be a brick wall or some higher ground or even better, a near view of hills or mountains. Inside the home it can be a painting of mountains or it can be a crystal geode. Failing all this, it is also a good idea to have bright lights. Fire element energy fuels the mountain and is very good for strengthening the mountain star.

118 NUMBER 4 BRINGS LITERARY & ROMANCE LUCK

The number 4 is the star of scholastic accomplishments and literary excellence. It signifies excellent writing skills and the attainment of exceptional academic success for those who can directly tap into its good energy. In the Constellation of nine stars, this number also stands for literary pursuits. All these positive attributes occur throughout the nine periods, but in varying strengths. In the current period of 8, the number 4 is not as vigorous as it can be. Nevertheless, it is still an indicator of romantic peach blossom luck.

The number 4 is strongest during the Period of 4. In the current period 8, the number 4 is not unlucky, but its strength is not as potent. When 4 transforms into a dead star, it can cause residents residing in the palace to be driven to severe mental stress, unless it is combined with an unaffiliated white star.

The number 4 tends to become a dead star during the Lower Periods of 7, 8 and 9. But when combined with 1, it comes alive and unleashes its positive benefits. So when water activates the wood of the number 4, it becomes energized and is suddenly strengthened, much like a dried plant hibernating and then springing to life in the Spring.

However, it is important not to have too much water, since excess water transforms the positive into negative. Wood dies when there is too much water. What hurts the number 4 star and causes it to "die" is metal energy. Hence the 4 when found in the metal sectors of West and Northwest is less potent than when it is found in the North.

The number 4 also signifies romance, although when there is excess water, the romance tends to be illicit in nature, leading to scandals and sordid problems associated with sexual infidelity. When the 4 combines with 1, it is already a good sign and it is not necessary to activate further except with movement and sounds, so placing a frequently used door in that sector or a moving fan will be sufficient to activate its good effects. It is better not to put too much water in a corner with the number 4, especially if it is the mountain star. This might lead to infidelity in a marriage.

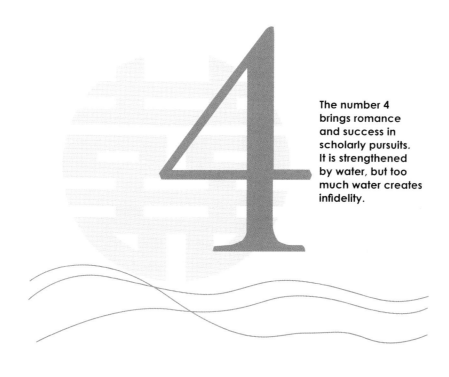

The number 4 brings romance and success in scholarly pursuits. It is strengthened by water, but too much water creates infidelity.

PURPLE 9 BRINGS
FUTURE PROSPERITY

The number 9 represents future prosperity. This is because 9 is the reigning number of the 20 year period of the next period (i.e. from the years 2024 to 2044) in the current millennium. Nine is the purple star and in the Constellation it is known as the right hand assistant.

Nine is often described as a big-hearted star. It nurtures and helps the matriarch care for the family. Nine expands and multiplies all good or bad fortune equally, especially when it is combined with an earth star number. When combined with 2 or 5, it expands their malevolence.

When combined with 8, it multiplies the good fortune. So with 9, it makes 8 even more auspicious, while with 2 and 5, it magnifies the misfortune brought by these two stars. The number 9 denotes the fire element and is especially auspicious when it occurs as a mountain star flown into any one of the earth sectors Southwest or Northeast.

But 9 can be regarded as a lucky number on its own. Much like 8, this number is a perennial favourite with the Chinese. In fact, amongst the Cantonese, they prefer 9 to 8, as the number 9 is also seen as the highest denomination number. The number 9 is a number that cannot change or be corrupted. Irrespective of how many times you multiply 9 by, the sum of its digits always add up to 9. So at its most yang and favourable, the number 9 brings fame and recognition, success and fruition. At its most negative, 9 brings arguments, fire and sickness associated with the eyes and the heart.

Displaying Nine Dragons is the most effective way of activating the good energy of the powerful nine.

120 THE UNLUCKY NUMBERS

The first of the unlucky numbers is the number 7 which in Period 8 is not a lucky number. In Period 8 it has become like a broken soldier, injured and dangerous. The star 7 should now be considered a vicious number indicating bloodshed and violence caused by metal. This is because 7 is a metal number and its color in the Constellation is red. So symbolically, it stands for a weapon (metal) that draws blood!

In terms of the member of the family, it signifies the youngest daughter. So when 7 is auspicious, it promises riches and it benefits the youngest child, especially the daughter of the family. Since it has turned nasty however, the number 7 causes robbery, betrayal, violence, and death and it brings danger to little girls. It can also signify loss of family members, imprisonment and accidents caused by fire. The best way to overcome the Number 7 star is with water, which exhausts its energy. Both yin and yang water are excellent for subduing the terrible energy of the 7 star.

The best cure for the number 7 star is a blue rhino, which should be placed where 7 flies to each year or month. This helps in reducing the danger of getting hurt, cheated and robbed as a result of the 7 appearing in your corner. Get a rhino that is about 8 inches in size. One with blue markings or is coloured blue to signify water is very effective. In 2008, the number 7 flies to the SW, so if your main door or bedroom is in the SW, you must have the blue rhino there. You can also get a miniature rhino and hang it on your handbag to protect against snatch thieves.

121 NUMBER 2 BRINGS ILLNESS LUCK

This is a number which is to be feared more as an annual and monthly star number than when it appears as a mountain or water star. It is the number that brings illness and when there is a concentration of 2s in the bedroom you occupy you are likely to get very ill. Sometimes the sickness can be so serious as to be fatal unless the necessary cures have been put into place to counter the intangible effect of the energy of the 2 star.

If your bedroom has the number 2 as the mountain star in the flying star chart of your home, it is likely that you could succumb easily to illness, bugs and flu viruses. During years and months when the number 2 also flies in to strengthen the natal mountain 2 star, the threat of illness becomes even more serious. It is thus a good idea to combat the number 2 mountain star, and this is best done in any of the following ways:

1. Place a six-rod all-metal windchime in the bedroom making sure it is not placed directly above your head when you sleep or sit in a chair. The best place to put this windchime is at the corner that corresponds to the location of the 2 star in the small tai chi of the room.
2. Place a brass or other metal wu lou in the corner of the room which corresponds to the location of the illness star. If this is not possible, then place the wu lou next to the bed inside the bedroom.
3. Do not inadvertently activate the mountain star with earth energy for instance by placing crystals or glass spheres in the corner of the illness star, since this will strengthen it.

4. Make sure you do not place lights or any kind of activating lamps in the corner of the illness star. Fire energy strengthens earth energy and the illness star 2 is an earth element star. Never use a salt lamp.
5. It is a good idea to sleep on a brass bed if the illness star afflicts the bedroom. A wooden bed is also a good idea.

The number 2 is known as a black star, and in the Constellation it is known as the Huge Door. The number 2 stands for the mother and when it shows its auspicious side, which is during the Period of 2, it brings great wealth and prosperity, high positions in the army and is especially benevolent towards mature women.

When it is negative however the number 2 causes the woman to suffer. It can also lead to premature widowhood, miscarriages, serious and fatal illness and stomach problems.

In the period of 8 the number 2 combines with the period number to create a sum of ten. So 2 is not considered a dangerous number in the current period. Instead, it possesses the potential of turning auspicious.

To dissolve the illness effects of 2 however, place the cures already recommended or simply hang a string of six metal coins at the palace having the number 2 influence. This strengthening of metal energy exhausts the earth of 2. The number 6 (and thus the 6 coins) represents Chien or big metal. The effect of 6 coins is extremely powerful since 6 signifies the power of heavenly forces. This is why we use the 6 rod windchime.

FIVE YELLOW IS BAD NEWS ALL THE WAY

The BAD luck numbers are generally regarded as the earth stars 2 and 5 as well as the hostile star 3. These numbers bring varying degrees of misfortune wherever and whenever they occur, either in the flying star natal charts, in the annual or monthly charts OR in the trigrams charts. Of these three numbers 5 is the most dangerous and is to be feared, 2 brings illness and 3 is the deadly star that brings a reversal of fortune causing severe problems and aggravations. The number 5 brings loss, tragedy and misfortune.

The number 5 has a pernicious effect.

This is the most troublesome of the nine numbers. Five is a yellow number and it is powerful because it is the center number of the original Lo Shu Square. Although it is known as the wicked star, nevertheless, in circumstances when it is benevolent, 5 brings exceptional prosperity luck. This occurs during the period of 5. It can also benefit those whose KUA number is 5.

Generally however, 5 is a very unfavourable star number that brings sickness, ill health and misfortune. To overcome its negative effects, you need a five element pagoda or a 6 rod windchime. These metal objects are powerful enough to exhaust the energy generated by the earth element of the number 5.

Remember that 5 is at its most harmful when it appears as an annual star (known as the *wu wang*) or when it is combined with the 9 star. This combination must be controlled wherever it occurs with a cure. The sound of metal caused by windchimes exhausts the Earth energy. The five element pagoda symbolically imprisons the earth energy inside the pagoda. Another strong method is to hang a metal curved knife high up near the ceiling, which symbolically destroys the number 5 star.

When both 5 and 2 occur together, you can use a brass windchime with six hollows rods but you will need a larger windchime to add strength. Or hang six windchimes. Or add 6 coins to make the cure stronger. Remember that when you hang windchimes you should hang them such that they are not suspended directly above anybody's head. Hang them near a wall rather than suspending just from the ceiling.

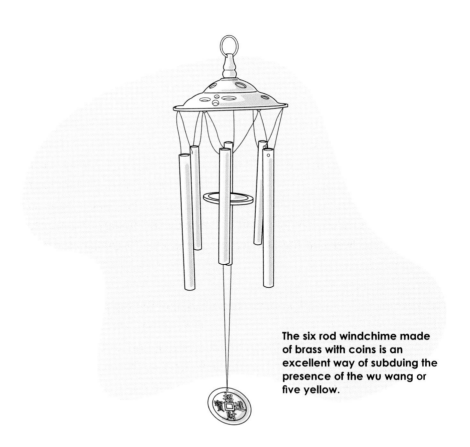

The six rod windchime made of brass with coins is an excellent way of subduing the presence of the wu wang or five yellow.

123 HOSTILE JADE 3 CAN BE DANGEROUS

The number 3 is generally regarded as a dangerous star. Three is the quarrelsome star that causes misunderstandings, disharmony and all kinds of obstacles to manifest. It has the power to aggravate situations and when it is strengthened, 3 brings lawsuits and court cases. In worst case scenarios it can bring violence and even death. In the constellation, it is known as the jade star and during its own period of 3, it brings wealth and prosperity and it benefits the eldest son of the family. But during periods 7 and 8, the number 3 is incredibly troublesome and inauspicious, bringing malicious gossip, injury to the limbs, the hands and legs, fingers and toes, and even worse, aggravations related to court cases, civil suits and run-ins with the authorities.

If you are experiencing a sudden onslaught of problems related to the law or with the civil and government authorities, you can be certain that you are being "hit" by the number three star. Most likely it is the annual and monthly star coming into your room or office or afflicting the location where your main entrance door is located. Internally within the body, the number 3 can create problems with the liver and the bladder, especially when it combines with the number 2 illness star.

The best way to overcome the negative aspects of the number 3 star is to shine a very bright light where it occurs. This means the corner where the flying star chart indicates its presence either as mountain, water, annual or monthly star. Painting the wall here a bright red is also very effective. The important thing is that the energy used to cure it must be quiet and silent fire energy, and then it is excellent for controlling its pernicious effect. In fact, fire cures for 3 are said to be exceptionally potent. If using bright lights is difficult, anything red will work such as a bright red curtain, or a painting that has predominantly red tones. But remember not to have any movement or sound. So do not place your fax machine, your copier machine or your printing machine here. Feng shui practitioners in the know are always wary of the number three star. And whether it afflicts you directly or not, the advice is to use red fire energy wherever it occurs.

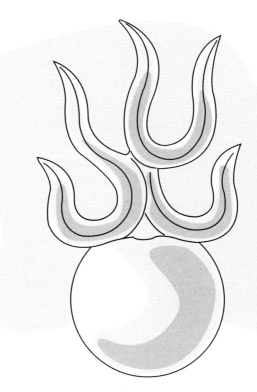

The Ksiddhigarbha Fire Ball with mantras is a very effective way of controlling the argumentative energy of the number 3 star.

124 SPECIALS THAT BRING AMAZING GOOD LUCK

In addition to interpreting the individual numbers within each of the grids, there are also "special situations" that bring excellent good fortune. This is when certain lucky combinations of numbers occur in the flying star chart bringing the potential for immense good fortune to manifest for the lucky residents. There are a number of such "specials" in the flying star charts of period 8 houses.

When you are fortunate enough to live in a house with these special combinations, and you activate the numbers correctly with the right kind of water and mountain features, activating the correct element or displaying a suitable auspicious object, the results can be quite spectacular.

Learning about these specials will help those building a new house, buying a new house or renovating their home to create the most auspicious design layout. This is an important part of Flying Star and signifies the practice at its most potent. Since we are in the Period of 8, feng shui practitioners should know about the specials of this period's flying star charts.

To make the best of them however, flying star specials must be successfully captured and activated, otherwise their benefits maybe not materialize. No matter what you hear or read elsewhere about not activating the different corners of your home using the theory of the five elements and the power of special auspicious symbols, this is what the feng shui formulas prescribe.

Activating the identified auspicious sectors in your house or office IS the practice of feng shui. Knowing the formula is of no use if you do not know how to activate the sectors, and how to make the fullest use of the numbers. Of course it is even worse when you activate them wrongly. Flying Star feng shui brings the potential for tremendous good fortune.

It is this promise that makes it so beneficial to study and to master feng shui. What I have written in this book makes Flying Star very accessible. Do not allow hearsay from others confuse you. Old feng shui masters often have great difficulty in adequately explaining the concepts behind their recommendations. So hopefully what is written here will help the reader understand feng shui recommendations that may be made to them.

Remember that feng shui is common sense but it also requires a certain scholarship as feng shui rules can be technical and are usually based on fundamental principles of Chinese scientific thinking. These incorporate the five elements, the principles of yin and yang as well as the respect for the intangible life force known as chi.

So feng shui recommendations must make sense to you. It must "feel" right and appeal to your own logical assessments and judgments. When you are in doubt, the best thing to do is to give it a rest for a few days before trying to analyse your feng shui or decide between options.

125 DIRECT & INDIRECT SPIRIT OF THE PERIOD

In every period, it is important to become so familiar with your house orientations that you can easily identify where the direct and indirect spirit of the period resides in your house. Every house and office building has two corners, which correspond to the direct and indirect spirit of the period. These two sectors of any building are where the wealth potential, and the best relationship and health luck can be activated. Only when the direct and indirect spirits are correctly activated can the wellbeing of residents in terms of health, wealth and happiness be assured throughout the entire period. This is one of the most potent "secrets" of the Flying Star system.

As we are living through the Period of 8, it is a good idea to immediately put into place these direct and indirect spirit safeguards in the home to ensure that the luck of your home is adequately taken care of for the full twenty years of Period 8 until the year 2024. If you do nothing else but just implement this measure, you will immediately feel the difference to your financials, to your relationships and to your health.

The way to ensure this safeguard is to follow the rule of placing a beautiful water feature in the place of the indirect spirit, and place a solid mountain feature in the place of the direct spirit. It is as simple as that!

During Period of 8, the Direct spirit resides in the NORTHEAST. This means that if yours is a Northeast house (i.e. it sits NE) you will enjoy tremendous good fortune. Your house reflects the essence of this Period's chi and is considered to be in perfect alignment with the cosmic chi of the current period.

This period corresponds to the KUA number 8 so people whose KUA number (under the Eight Mansions formula) is 8 will enjoy excellent luck in such a house as well as all through the period. Those with KUA number 2 also benefit, as 2 adds up to ten with the number 8 thereby creating the completion chi of the sum of ten. Women whose KUA number is 5 also benefit from this period's energy, as 5 for women translates into 8. Likewise for men as well because their KUA then becomes 2 and this gives them the sum of ten completion advantage.

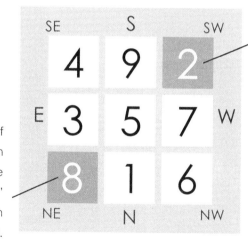

The Indirect Spirit of Period 8 resides in the SW. Activate with "water" for good wealth luck.

The Direct Spirit of Period 8 resides in the NE. Activate with "mountain" for good health and relationships.

126 ACTIVATING DIRECT & INDIRECT SPIRIT

To activate the direct spirit, place a solid wall, or big stones or crystals in the NE of your house. If this also happens to be the back of your house, it is REALLY excellent and is perfect feng shui!

As an additional tip, take note that it is better to sit NE1 (which means your house faces SW1) than it is to have the house sit NE2 or 3. This is because in the flying star chart, when your house sits NE1, the mountain star 8 is located at the back of the house. Then placing a mountain feature at the back here will be automatically activating the auspicious mountain star as well. However note that irrespective of what direction your house faces, you should place a mountain feature in the NE to activate the direct spirit of your house.

When you have the presence of a "mountain" in the Northeast, the energy of the current period is in place to bring you amazing relationship and health luck. This is the key that unlocks extreme good fortune as it brings you the help of influential people. Your wellness will ensure you stay fit enough to carry through whatever you may be working on. When the NE has a mountain, you will be activating the cosmic chi of the period. The benefits are enormous!

Meanwhile, the indirect spirit resides in the Southwest during Period 8.

So you should focus on placing a water feature such as a swimming pool or a fishpond in the Southwest sector of your house. Doing this is sure to bring you wealth and income growth luck in abundance. If this SW sector also corresponds to the front of your house, or to where your water star 8 of your flying star chart resides, then you will get a multiplied advantage.

This is the case if your house is facing the Southwest 1 direction. This is what I describe as very premier and superior feng shui. But always remember the rules of water feng shui. For example, when building your water feature, be it a pond or a pool, you should really ensure that the water is flowing inwards and not outwards. Let water (wealth) flow towards you and not away from you. Your water feature must also not be so large as to overwhelm your house. Use indoor water features if you live in apartments or condominiums.

127 MONTH AND DAY CHARTS

I t is beneficial to study the day and hour influences of energy and add these to your reading, although it is not strictly necessary for the amateur practitioner to do so. This is however very easy to learn.

All you need is to cast the monthly and daily Lo Shu charts. When you look into the Chinese Almanac's thousand year calendar, one of the pieces of information you will find is the Lo Shu number of each day and also every hour of each day. This is the reigning number of that microcosm of time. Simply by placing the Lo Shu number in the center of a 3X3 Lo shu chart, you can instantly generate the complete Lo Shu chart of that particular month or day. In my annual FENG SHUI DIARY I have included the Lo Shu numbers of each day.

SE	S	SW
2	8	1
E 1	4	6 W
7	9	5
NE	N	NW

Month with the Lo Shu number 4, so this is the chart for that month.

SE	S	SW
1	6	8
E 9	2	4 W
5	7	3
NE	N	NW

Day with the Lo Shu number 2, so this is the number in the center of the chart.

CHANGING STRENGTH OF NUMBERS

Every numbers possesses intrinsic attributes that indicate specific types of good fortune or misfortune, but it is necessary to take note of their relative strength in different periods. The strength of numbers change over time so we take note of the strong and weak numbers during the current period of 8. The six qualities of chi in Flying Star analysis reflect the strength and quality of each of the numbers. In each period, numbers represent different types of chi and we factor this into our analysis. Basically we take note of numbers with strong chi energy and avoid numbers that signify death and decline.

In the period of 8, the strength of the number 8 is at its height, so this is a brilliant number. On the other hand, the number 7 is at its weakest. This is because the number of the immediately previous period is always the weakest. This is why all period 7 houses are now described as having very weak chi energy. And even though the number 7 now signifies violence and burglary luck, its energy is weak and so it can be overcome more easily.

The number 6 was weak during the previous period and by the start of period 8 was considered a number with dead chi, but it can be easily revived and recover its strength, so this auspicious number is considered to have the potential to be relatively strong. The number 9 is strong. The numbers 2 and 5, which bring misfortune luck, are strong in the current period of 8, as both are earth numbers and this is an earth period. The numbers 3 and 4 are strong numbers as these are wood numbers, which control earth. However, while 3 is a quarrelsome number, 4 is the number of love.

The numbers also have six types of chi energy, three of which are positive and three are negative. The three types of positive chi are:

1. **Ripening Chi** - also known as prosperity or wang chi − it is good energy to activate.

   When the mountain star is a number that represents wang chi, and it is activated by nearby mountains in the direction indicated by its placement in the chart, these mountains will bring enormous good fortune. When there are no mountains look out for tall buildings that can take the place of mountains. When even this is nowhere to be found hang a painting of mountains in the part of the house which has this auspicious mountain star. Your fortunes are sure to improve by leaps and bounds. This is because the meaning of this kind of chi is that "your luck has ripened, it has arrived!"

   In the same way, when the water star of any sector has the number which indicates ripening chi of that period, it suggests the potential for great wealth to arrive very quickly. The chi has to be activated by the presence of real water, and the water should be yang; it should be moving, clean and better yet have some fish swimming in it. There is no better energizer than "alive" water. In any period, it is the number of the period that represents the ripening chi. So in the Period of 8, the number that represents ripening chi is the number 8.

GROWING CHI

Growing Chi: This is also referred to as sheng chi – this is energy that is growing stronger, expanding, about to blossom. This number possesses chi that signifies coming good fortune. This can mean a whole variety of things – promotion at work, upward mobility in one's career luck, a major political appointment, an offer you cannot refuse, anything at all that can qualify to be described as making progress. In business it can suggest getting a major infusion of cash, or an attractive takeover offer or a landing a major new contract.

Many feng shui masters view sheng chi with greater favour than ripening chi as growth energy always has excellent feng shui connotations. When your life or your career is growing there is a presumption that the best is yet to come.

When the mountain star has this number, it means that recognition is just ground the corner. When the water star has this number it means a cash windfall is about to come your way. But for these things to happen, both the mountain and water star must be activated. In the period of 8, the number which represents sheng chi is the number 9, which indicates coming prosperity.

IMPROVING CHI

Improving chi: This is the number which indicates that luck is improving because all the obstacles confronting you are weakening. Luck has not arrived but there are good signs of improvement. This number should not be energized − this is because the energy of this number is weak, and activating it will only cause it to retreat. So improving chi numbers should be left alone. The number that represents improving chi in the Period of 8 is the number 1. This kind of chi is akin to distant prosperity. It is a very long-term type of good energy. For those of you who are still in your teens however this number becomes important as it opens the door to future prosperity for you. The time to activate the number 1 is during the period of 9.

In the current period just view the number 1 favourably and go for the slow and steady approach. Bide your time and work at preparing yourself for good energy to eventually blossom.

132 THREE TYPES OF NEGATIVE CHI ENERGY

The three types of negative chi energy are:

1. **Declining Chi**: This is the number which suggests that luck is waning, energy is weakening and obstacles to success are piling up. Luck is slipping away. When the mountain star has this number, it indicates that power and influence are on the decline. Those who do not want to lose their positions in high office must make sure they do not stay in a room where the mountain star is this number. Similarly, for those in business and going through hard times, if they want their companies to survive, they must make very sure they do not stay in a room where the water star shows this number. And they should not live in a house where the water star at the facing palace has this number. Declining fortunes is truly painful to experience, so do take note and adopt strong precautions.

   In the Period of 8 the number of declining chi is 7. I have been urging everyone to change their homes into Period 8 homes as at least half the homes belonging to Period 7 have the double water and mountain star 7 at the facing palace. This has the potential to cause some major disasters. Hence better to change to Period 8.

2. **Dead Chi**: This is the number that suggests danger and decay. It is also known as Si chi Various manifestations of bad luck are visited upon those affected by the number that signifies dead chi during the current period There is no more life and no more progress. The energy has simply died. It is necessary to try to move out of rooms afflicted by dead chi numbers (manifested as either water or mountain stars). BUT the good news is that

you can bring the number to life again! You can do this very easily by using the element cycles.

In the period of 8, the number that signifies dead chi is the number 6. To bring this number to life, all you need is to use the productive cycle of the five elements. So use earth energy i.e. place boulders and crystals to revive the number 6. Shine a bright light at the place where the 6 occurs to strengthen earth energy and 6 magically revives. Just note that when energizing dead chi numbers, you must never overdo things. Moderation is required.

3. **Killing Chi**: This is shar chi – the most powerfully destructive chi. It is necessary to watch out for these harmful star numbers as they are negative and strong at the same time! When the mountain star is a number, that signifies shar chi in the current period, it can cause sudden reversals of fortune and even death. Other manifestations are becoming a victim of murder, sickness or suicide. The numbers that signify killing chi in the Period of 8 are the numbers 2, 3 and 5. As these are intrinsically very unlucky and troublesome numbers anyway, it is necessary to be ever watchful about them when they appear. Use feng shui cures to press down or at least control these numbers where they appear.

The best way to suppress the killing energy of 2 and 5 is to use metal windchimes and the best way to suppress the killing energy of 3 is to use the colour red. But it should be a red that is yin (i.e. silent) so red curtains, red paintings or red lights would do the job. Because 3 is also the quarrelsome star, it is important not to activate it with noise or moving objects.

133 THE NINE CYCLES OF CHI

The information contained in the table here summarizes the chi energy of the numbers in different periods and is very similar to the nine cycles of chi manifested in houses built in different periods. The nine cycles of chi looks at the different Period houses and assigns different strength to their chi.

This takes account of the chi of any house. This is one of the most closely guarded secrets in the application of Flying Star feng shui. When you study how the chi of houses wax and wane from period to period, you will realize that the chi of houses can get exhausted unless the chi is properly reenergized.

How can we bring new life to old houses that suffer from exhausted chi? It must be obvious that when the chi of any abode is tired or even dead, residents living in such houses cannot benefit.

So the secret of Flying Star is that Chi must always be replenished.

This is what gives strength to one's good fortune. This is what sustains family fortunes. When the chi of the family abode is regularly revitalized, family fortunes stay intact and even expand from one generation to the next. When the chi of family homes is allowed to dwindle and die, the fortunes of the family also get dispersed. Descendants lose their closeness to the family.

The best way to revitalise energy is with plenty of noise. Using the lion dance, throwing a big party and arranging an extensive prayer offering ritual (puja) are some of the ways of activating stagnant chi. Fire up your home with a yang chi bath and you will feel the difference immediately.

PERIOD	PERIOD #	RIPENING	GROWING	IMPROVING	DECLINING	DEAD	KILLING
UPPER	1	1	2	3	9	6, 7	5, 7
UPPER	2	2	3	4	1	9, 6	5, 7
UPPER	3	3	4	5	2	1, 6	7
MIDDLE	4	4	5	6	3	2, 8	2, 7
MIDDLE	5	5	6	7	4	2, 3	2, 3
MIDDLE	6	6	7	8	5	4, 9	2, 3
LOWER	7	7	8	9	6	1, 4	2, 3, 5
LOWER	8	8	9	1	7	4, 6	2,3,5
LOWER	9	9	1	2	8	4, 6	3,5.7

Table of Chi Energy of the Numbers 1 to 9 in the Nine Periods.

134 REVITALISING CHI

This means making sure the house is well-maintained and kept in good condition. Everything in the house should work, from the plumbing to the electricity. Bulbs should never be left unchanged and there should be no wilting flowers left in vases. Revitalizing also means replenishing yang energy to keep the house chi alive and active. When abandoned and left to rot, houses literally die, yang energy seeps out, wilts, and then the energy of the house grows yin until finally it goes to sleep completely! That is when yin spirit formation takes place to the detriment of residents.

Even if you do not know Flying Star, if you frequently introduce movement, change, repaint jobs, small renovations to your home, this alone revitalizes it and brings in fresh strong chi that can only benefit residents. So people who regularly make changes to their home are actually practicing excellent feng shui without knowing it.

Re-energizing your feng shui is really good for health and for bringing opportunities to all areas of your life. It is for this reason that I always do something with my home every year. And also why I hold a Chinese New Year party each new year − to bring in precious yang chi that keeps my home bustling with happiness, activity, noise and good health. Knowing Flying Star enables me to make certain I keep all auspicious flying stars nicely activated, and all bad stars under control.

This is why I enjoy feng shui so much, and why I am so passionate about passing on my excellent results to readers.

Not simply the knowledge and the methodology of feng shui, but, more importantly the attitude towards its practice. Harmony in the home can do with a helping hand from feng shui, but one's attitude must be positive.

Plus here's another secret which I am burying deep into this book – and that is to always think big when you make feng shui adjustments or enhancements. Have big expectations and big aspirations. This way you will be seriously strengthening the feng shui energy. I intend to write a whole book just on this subject because it is such a vital part of why feng shui has worked so gloriously well for me! It is also important to stay relaxed at all times – you must never be obsessive or dogmatic in the practice of feng shui. Stay cool always.

The moment you get uptight about feng shui, or allow some so called master to scare you, the fun (and effectiveness) is taken out of feng shui. More significantly, it sets you into a negative spiral and it will play havoc with your mind, and as a result, with your feng shui also. Always be very aware of commercial feng shui con-men who are really good at marketing themselves by selling others short. They do nothing but criticize other practitioners' feng shui. In my experience I have always found those whose knowledge to be deep and meaningful are usually the most humble of all. All the true and genuine feng shui masters I have ever met (and believe me, I have met many) are always full of good humour, are extremely humble and are understated. They never ever criticize other practitioners. Truly from them I leant more than feng shui! I learnt the huge and immense power of thinking good positive thoughts and I also learnt how to think big and how to rejoice in the success of others.

So practice feng shui with a big heart and all your expectations will materialize gloriously for you.

DIFFERENT PERIOD HOUSES

The tips summarized here offer practical references based on the Nine Cycles of Chi. From these you can get a feel for houses built in different periods.

1. Houses built during Periods 1, 6 and 8 have strong chi while houses built during Periods 2 and 5 tend to be weak. Period 1, 6 and 8 houses enjoy good chi in many other periods. Period 2 and 5 houses tend to have dead chi in most other periods. So if you purchase a house built in Period 2 or 5, go all out to revitalize its chi and change its period by undertaking massive renovations – lots of banging and knocking.

2. The chi of all houses decline in the period that comes immediately after the period in which they were built. Thus all Period 7 houses suffered a massive decline in energy from Feb 4th 2004 onwards, because this was the day when Period 8 started.

3. During Period 8, no houses except Period 7 houses suffer from dead energy. Houses built in periods 1, 2, 3, 4, 5 and 6 enjoy good energy. Only Period 7 houses suffer from declining energy. Thus I am strongly recommending that everyone presently living in a Period of 7 house or building should make plans to change to a Period 8 house. In fact, this is the prime motivation for my writing this advanced book of feng shui. Unless you change the period of your house, the probability of you suffering misfortune or going into a decline is sure to happen.

136 FLYING STAR COMBINATIONS

More important than understanding single numbers is to correctly interpret combinations of numbers., which refer to the following:

- Combinations of Mountain Star with Period Star
- Combinations of Water Star with Mountain Star
- Combinations of Period Star with Water Star
- Combinations of Annual and Month Stars

Different practitioners place different emphasis on these combinations. You will find that there are those who look only at the Mountain and Water Stars. They tend to downplay the importance of the Period Star and their argument is that no one's luck can be consistently good or bad for as long as twenty years. So to them it is the Water and Mountains Stars and how these react to the Annual and Month Stars that give a really true picture of chi distribution in any house.

Equally, many masters look at the Period and Water Stars as well as the Period and Mountain combinations. This group considers it ridiculous that the Period Stars are ignored, and I tend to agree. In my analysis of Flying Star charts, I actually study all aspects and all dimensions and try to take a wholistic view on what the numbers are telling me. Sometimes I find that certain combinations of numbers just jump up at me, especially when the surrounding environment – the roads and mountains, buildings and rivers - all point to exciting feng shui potential. Other times because I am searching for specific manifestations of bad combinations to explain why a friend or a family is having a spate of bad luck, then I look to find what I am searching for.

So I prefer to adopt a less dogmatic approach, preferring to keep an open mind and to allow for a certain amount of flexibility of possibilities. I do urge you to do the same. It is really beneficial to remember that feng shui is an ancient practice, which we are all trying to transplant into a thoroughly modern environment. So do allow that interpretations of the numbers - in as far as aspirations success, happiness, love and so forth - will have different connotations today then they did a thousand years ago in old China!

In terms of just looking at the numbers, perhaps the initial starting point would be to look out for some of the important combinations, and these can be summarized in the following pages under auspicious and inauspicious combinations.

137 AUSPICIOUS NUMBER COMBINATIONS

The combinations that spell wealth luck are indicated by the auspicious white numbers 1, 6 and 8 occurring together in a single palace. The three stars – main star, water star and mountain star - make up this combination of numbers.

Firstly, it is the white stars that are always the most auspicious, and in the Lower Period (i.e. the present period) the number 8 is the major white star. The number 1 is the supporting star, while the number 6 is the declining white star. This gives you an idea of the strength of their chi. Note therefore how incredibly important the number 8 is in the current period that lasts until 2024.

Secondly, there is a combination that indicates the potential for marriage, the birth of a child or a longevity birthday celebration. These events are collectively referred to as happiness occasions or in Chinese *hei see*. When the bedroom or main door is located in a palace with the combination of 4 and 1, with the 4 being the mountain star and 1 being the water star, it indicates happiness occasions. In modern day feng shui, such occasions can also be extended to college graduation as well as the son or daughter of the family starting out on their career.

Thirdly, take note of the doubles. This indicates the double 8 in the Period of 8. This combination refers to mountain and water stars both being 8. It is best when the double 8 is at the Facing Palace where the main door is located OR at the back door in the sitting palace. To activate this combination, place water near the door and have a view of a mountain further away. This way you capture both the mountain and water. If the mountain is too near (i.e. if there is a wall near to the entrance) and there is also water nearby then the mountain is said to have fallen into the water. This situation means that the residents will become rich but they could also lose their good name, health or popularity. Doubles either in front or behind always benefit from the presence of real water and real mountains. A great way to energize the double 8 either behind or in front is to create a man made waterfall, i.e. a mountain where water slowly trickles down its sides. As long as the water does not "drown" the mountain, the structure will be auspicious.

Fourthly, take note of additional meanings to the combinations of the Main Star with the water star that are auspicious when present in all the palaces. Note the first number is the main number and the second number is the water star number.

- 1/4 or 4/1 means success in examinations and scholarly pursuits. Rooms with such combinations should be given to your college-going children.
- 6/8 means success in business, while 8/6 means scholarly pursuits bringing recognition and influence.
- 4/6 means talent and fame that take residents very far
- 8/9 means a happy family with lots of happiness occasions
- 9/8 means fame with prosperity and financial success
- 2/8 in the Northwest means great wealth and success for the patriarch. This is a sum of ten combination.
- 3/1 in the West means many good descendants who bring honor and wealth to the family.
- Combinations of 1/6, 1/1, 1/8. 6/4, 6/6 and 8/8 all mean good fortune and great health. In the central palace, also known as the "heavenly heart", the presence of these numbers benefit the whole family. Interactions in specific rooms affect activities in those rooms and benefit those residing there.

Fifthly, there are other special combinations that suggest auspicious potential especially when properly activated. These "specials" take us deeper into Flying Star interpretations and I have included them in the next four sections. These advanced readings include the four sets of Ho Tu numbers, the three sets of the parent string numbers, and so forth. Other combinations take account of the flight path of the stars and the strength of yin and yang of the numbers. For the moment, it is sufficient to attain a certain familiarity with the common combinations first. These are easy to spot and easy to activate.

Results are felt very fast and this should surely inspire you to move to the next level of learning.

These are the three white numbers which create an auspicious combination.

COMBINATION 2 with 5 BRINGS LOSS

The combination that indicates the presence of negative chi, severe illness, loss, accidents and misfortunes is the combination of the star numbers 2 and 5, especially when it occurs as either Mountain or Water Star. The number 2 star is more deadly when it makes its appearance as the Mountain Star. Here are some useful pointers to note in your interpretation of these numbers in the flying star chart.

When the combination involves a Main Star the effect of the 5 is said to be lessened marginally. When the Mountain Star is 5, it indicates loss of a loved one, an important friend, a highly valued relationship or a loss of job. When the Mountain Star is 2, it indicates severe illness, going into hospital, contracting a disease, having an operation or the discovery that one is suffering from a serious or terminal disease.

When the Water Star is 5, it indicates a loss of wealth, declining profits and severe financial problems. Sometimes it indicates loss of income and status. When the Water Star is 2, it suggests mental illness, succumbing to pressure and an inability to cope with finances – usually this means a severe cash bind that leads to illness or a breakdown.

These two numbers 2 and 5 are indeed to be feared, and they create enormous mischief to residents when they fly into the facing palace. This is the part of the house where the main front door into the home is located. They also cause problems when they are inside your bedroom. When they are elsewhere in your home, you do not need to worry about them too much.

The impact of the 2 and 5 become more fatal when the annual 5 or annual 2 also fly in to strengthen the combination. I simply cannot over stress the danger of such a situation. The impact of the 5's or 2's all congregated in one palace is like having a bomb in there!

The best way to cope with the 5/2 disastrous combinations is simply to move out of any room occupied by these numbers. Use that room as a storeroom, because this way you are imprisoning the bad stars. I have discovered this to be an excellent way of coping with these horrible stars. Keep them locked up!

Another excellent cure I find very effective are brass windchimes. These exhaust the afflicted chi of the 5 and the 2. Metal coins placed in a row above doorways are also favoured by flying star experts from Hong Kong. Indeed in Hong Kong, many of the homes of the local tycoons have paintings of mountains made of metal. These are effective in keeping the 2 and 5 under wraps.

There is danger indicated when you encounter the troublesome doubles i.e. the double 5s and double 2s. These can easily extend into triples when we include the annual and monthly stars, so do strenuously avoid the doubles. The combination can be Main Star with either Water or Mountain Star, or it could be Water and Mountain. It is vital to use the windchime or coin cure to exhaust the energy of the double 2s and 5s. If one sleeps or works in a sector that is afflicted by these numbers, note that the 2s will bring severe sickness while the 5s will bring loss or accidents.

139   THE DANGER OF 3 with 2

The combination of 3/2 or 2/3 is exceptionally dangerous. This is the quarrelsome combination and wherever it is present, it sows discord and dissent. More to the point, anytime the 3 appears it brings aggravations of the most serious kind – litigations, run-ins with the law and authorities and even being sued and taken to court. If you are a doctor, it might bring a malpractice suit; if you are a prominent civil servant, it might bring anti-corruption charges – that kind of aggravation. Inland revenue might come after you or worse still, you might even get arrested and imprisoned. It is very likely that Paris Hilton got hit by the number 3 star and that caused her to have to go to jail in June 2007. In short, the number 3, when strong enough, can bring sudden disaster into your life.

The combination of 3 and 2 must never get activated either by noise or activity. The more the combination gets activated, the higher will be the likelihood of residents encountering problems with the authorities, bureaucracy and with the legal system and the Courts. Litigation becomes a problem there will be a great deal of disharmony. The best way to overcome the energy of the 3/2 combination is to use fire energy, but it must be a silent fire. So it can be a red lamp which does not make noise.

The red exhausts the three without activating it. Some practitioners do not like using red because they say it strengthens the sickness star 2, since fire makes earth in the element cycle, but I have discovered that red always works. Two other cures I have used with great success are solid crystal balls and yin water. Place six round crystal balls in the afflicted palace to promote harmony. Or place an urn or a big vase filled with non-moving water. The Chinese word for vase is *ping*, and this also means peace. That is why the Chinese are so fond of ceramic vases. In any sector, they signify harmony of relations. When you have the 3 present, you must really avoid hanging metal windchimes, clocks or other moving objects. Also, do not have the radio or TV set placed there as this will activate the 3, making it very strong indeed.

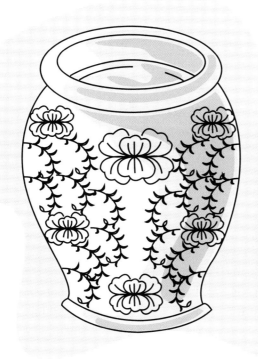

The vase is a symbol of peace and harmony. When filled with yin water it has the ability to create calmness in the atmosphere. Filled with rice and other auspicious things, it can become a wealth vase attracting abundance. The vase is an excellent cure for the #3 star.

140 THE 5 AND 9 MAGNIFIES MISFORTUNES

The combination of 5/9 or 9/5 is definitely to be feared because here the 9 multiplies the 5, so the danger of the five yellow is strengthened. This is a combination that represents the very powerful *wu wang*. The fire energy of 9 magnifies the fatal earth energy of 5 and where it occurs, this combination creates severe blocks to success.

This combination can also cause accidents that lead to fairly serious injuries. The best way to control this combination is by using metal windchimes. You will need windchimes with 6 hollow rods as this tool offers an added boost of metal represented by the number 6. If the 5 Mountain Star with the 9 Water Star afflicts your bedroom, the effect is that your relationship with each other and with others will be seriously harmed by bad feng shui in your bedroom – often bad enough to cause a split. The Mountain star here is being strengthened by the Water Star, so outsiders can and will use their money to harm you both.

If the Water Star is 5 and the Mountain Star is 9, you will suffer a loss of profits or you might find that your business or your wealth will be stolen from you. Unless you overcome the effect of this combination by placing a large five-element pagoda in the afflicted sector you will find it hard to overcome the full import of bad feng shui. If one of the cures is insufficient, use several, as the five element pagoda is an excellent remedy.

141 SUMMARY OF BAD COMBINATIONS

Condensed here is a summary of the inauspicious combinations in a flying star chart. The meanings apply to the sectors of the home or office that is afflicted by these combinations. Note that when the combination is Mountain Star/Water Star, the impact of the negativity will be extra strong and cures are a must. When the first number refers to the Main Star and the second number is either the Water or Mountain Star, the effect is not so strong.

- 7/9 indicates problems caused by political intrigues. Use yin water in a maroon vase.
- 2/5 or 5/2 means severe illness. Use metal windchimes or gold coins to overcome − you can also use the five element pagoda.
- 3/7 mean loss of fortunes through robbery or legal hassle. Use yin fire energy such as red cloth.
- 9/7 means fire caused by human activity. Use Yin water in a golden phoenix vase.
- 2/7 means fire caused by natural occurrence. Use yin water in a vase. You should also display a blue rhino.
- 5/5 means severe illness. Control with metal windchimes.
- 5/9 means accidents leading to hospitalization or death. Use metal windchimes as well as a five element pagoda.
- 7/6 or 6/7 means armed robbery leading to injury. Use yin water in a dragon vase. Also use the blue rhino.
- 7/3 betrayal, trickery and intrigue at work. Be careful. Use glitter lights to overcome. Also use the rooster.

- 3/7 brings illness caused by worry and anxieties. Victim of politics. Use glitter lights or invite in the rooster image.
- 6/9 illness of internal organs. Older residents at risk. Place wu lou in the room.
- 7/5 or 9/5 means terminal illness. Place wu lou in the room.
- 8/4 or 3/8 means unhealthy children always sick. Use six coins placed over entrance.
- 2/9 means obstacles in business ventures – use metal bells to overcome. Invite Kuan Kung into the house.
- 2/3 indicates too many mouths to feed. Use yin water in a vase. Also use the Ksiddhigarbha fireball.

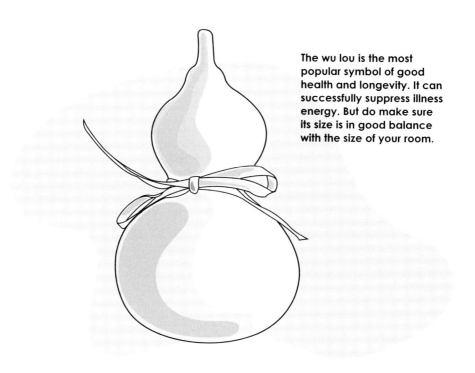

The wu lou is the most popular symbol of good health and longevity. It can successfully suppress illness energy. But do make sure its size is in good balance with the size of your room.

142 IMPACT OF THE ELEMENTS

It is necessary to take note of the elements of the numbers. Thus 1 is water. 2 is earth, 3 is wood, 4 is wood, 5 is earth, 6 is metal, 7 is metal, 8 is earth, and 9 is fire. Take note of these number/element combinations and commit them to memory if you wish to become a good feng shui practitioner.

1. Each direction has an element. North is water, Southwest is earth, Southeast is wood, East is wood, the center is Earth, Northwest is metal, West is metal, Northeast is earth, and South is fire. When a number flies into a corner, always think "what element is flying into which element" and then ask yourself if the incoming element is enhancing, exhausting or destroying the element of the palace or sector. This alone offers you clues on whether the number flying into any sector is good or bad for the sector in that year and month.

2. The result or outcome of numbers coming into a sector can be auspicious or inauspicious. If they are inauspicious they can always be corrected! How? With the correct use of a remedy element, they always work.

3. The combinations of Water and Mountain Stars can be analyzed to indicate if they are auspicious or inauspicious. Here you can see which star is stronger.

4. Never forget the impact of the TIME stars. Each, day, month, year and each 20 year period has different reigning Lo Shu numbers that can be expanded into charts. These time stars exert their influence on the palaces. When there

is a concentration of BAD stars on a particular day or month, any negative or positive effect is considerably strengthened. Based on this, combinations are never always good and seldom always bad. It depends on other stars combining with them.

5.   Finally, when bad stars or good stars combine, they often need a catalyst - an external feature or structure - to trigger an effect. Like karma ripening at a particular moment in time. Thus external forms and structures combine with flying star to speed up good and bad effects. Similarly, symbolic decorative pieces have the same triggering effect. So when a bad annual star flies into a sector with unlucky natal chart numbers, bad luck gets triggered much faster when that affected palace is also being hurt by a physical poison arrow.

DIRECTIONS AND ELEMENTS

143 FACTORS THAT DETERMINE OUTCOMES

When analyzing flying star charts, always take note that every combination of numbers can have good as well as bad outcomes. The outcomes depend on four factors:

1. whether or not the numbers have been effectively activated either with elements or symbols that magnify their energy. Symbols play a big role in activating.
2. whether or not the numbers are in their positive or negative period cycle – this means how strong their chi is as well as the quality of their chi in the current period. Remember that numbers have different strengths in different periods.
3. whether or not the element of the incoming stars (i.e. the Water and Mountain Stars) strengthen or weaken the palace they occupy. There are remedies for bad stars and energizers for good stars and these are usually based on the application of the element cycles. Mainly we use the productive cycle to energize and the exhaustive cycle to remedy.

Note that a seriously bad combination of numbers should be kept unused and unactivated. Remedies may reduce ill effects but they cannot completely overcome, especially when an incoming annual or monthly visiting star has an evil nature. So always watch annual and monthly stars! When environmental features such as a straight oncoming road, a tall building or heavy and fast moving traffic add fuel to the bad stars, the results can be tragic.

144 MOUNTAIN & WATER STAR COMBINATIONS

The most important combination of numbers within a flying star chart is the Mountain and Water Star combination. These two stars define the quality of chi energy in the sector they occupy. Thus in addition to the meaning of the individual numbers, the combination of the two stars offer additional insights which, in the hands of an experienced feng shui expert, reveal a wealth of additional meanings.

Of the two stars, the Water Star exerts the most influence mainly because it signifies all the material aspects of life. Thus the Water Star indicates wealth luck and when there is a good Water Star, the presence of real water and a good chunk of yang energy will energize it, making it come alive with goodies! A good wealth star brings wealth to residents who live within its vicinity.

The Mountain Star always brings indications of health luck and relationships luck. Here we are talking not merely about relationships between lovers and spouses.

The scope of the Mountain Star is broad based. It also covers relationships between partners, business associates, siblings, and so forth. If you think about your life, you realize that happiness basically depends on the quality of all the relationships in your life. Thus from this perspective, the Mountain Star is in many ways even more important than the Water Star. However, in terms of chi strength, it is the Water Star that is more powerful as it exerts greater influence than the Mountain Star. In the current period of 8, however, the Mountain Star has become extremely important and strong.

145 MOUNTAIN STAR 1 COMBINATIONS

When the mountain star is 1, relationship luck is good. The number 1 is an auspicious number bringing excellent work relationships and the possibility of income enhancement arising from one's networking. When the mountain star is enhanced by a quartz crystal cluster, the mountain star gets activated bringing auspicious relationship luck and excellent good health.

When the Mountain Star 1 combines with a Water Star 2, there could be marriage problems as well as the danger of loss of relationships and of one's source of income. The 2 water star brings illness associated with money worries. Meanwhile, the 2 water star corrupts the 1 mountain star and this manifests the water in the mountain as a sign of grave danger; it indicates the mountain star has fallen into water – a bad sign indeed. You can use plants to exhaust the water in this sector.

When the Mountain Star is 1 and the Water Star is 3, wealth and fame luck are indicated. However, do note that the 3 water star in itself is dangerous since this is the hostile star. Combined with the 1 Mountain Star however, it becomes benevolent. Use water to enhance this combination and water plants to add to its luster. Note that prosperity luck is good, but if you don't have the karma/luck to live in this home, it might cause you to change residence.

When the Mountain Star is 1 and the Water Star is 4, there is political good fortune so there is the potential of great power for the family. Residents will enjoy media and publicity luck. Romance is also possible for younger members of the family. Use slow moving water to enhance, but not too much.

When the Mountain Star is 1 and the Water Star is 5 there will be health problems dealing with the kidney. It is important to hang a windchime or place a five element pagoda here. When the Mountain Star is 1 and the Water Star is 6, residents will be perceived as intelligent with great commercial skills, so this is a very auspicious combination. It brings good name and good reputation to the family.

When the Mountain Star is 1 and the Water Star is 7, this used to mean good fortune in the just ended period of 7, but now in Period 8, it means loss and danger. The sector needs a water feature to control the Water Star 7 which brings loss through being cheated or burgled.

When the Mountain Star is 1 and the Water Star is 8, there is excellent wealth luck in Period 8 – this is a most auspicious indication as the Water Star 8 is incredibly lucky. Wherever the Water Star 8 appears, it is really important to activate it with the presence of water – preferably a pond or pool dug out from the ground.

When the Mountain Star is 1 and the Water Star is 9 it is a good combination but it can turn bad when the wu wang 5 flies in either as the annual or the month star. This combination is best left alone.

146 MOUNTAIN STAR 2 COMBINATIONS

When the Mountain Star is 2, it brings severe ill health. Since the Mountain Star stands for health and the number 2 is the sickness star, this can potentially be a very harmful indication. It is vital to place a metal windchime here, and possibly have this supplemented with an eight immortal wu lou placed prominently in the corner where it occurs.

When it combines with the Water Star 1, it indicates that the matriarch of the household will be too strong and this could lead to marital problems. It is necessary to enlarge the store of metal chi energy.

When it combines with the 3 Water Star, there will be arguments and misunderstandings of the most severe kind. Back stabbing, intense hatred or legal disputes are likely to manifest. So this is an inauspicious combination. Any sector occupied by this 2 and 3 combination should be regarded as a very dangerous sector to live or work in. The best cure is to place something bright red here. It can be tablecloths, a feature wall painted red, scatter cushions in bright vermillion OR best of all, a Laughing Buddha image wearing red robes. Since it is the water star that is the hostile 3 here, the danger is a loss of wealth. With the 2 as the Mountain Star, health problems develop. This becomes a very inauspicious location that is best avoided.

When it combines with the 4 Water Star, there could be problems between young wives and their mothers-in-law. Disharmony sets in very quickly and the cure is to do as little as possible together. Feng shui can help reduce aggravations but cannot do away with it altogether, so the best solution here is to skillfully avoid each other.

When the Mountain Star 2 combines with the Water Star 5, it is extremely inauspicious suggesting even total loss and sheer catastrophe. This is one of the most dangerous combinations in Flying Star. When the annual 5 flies in, anyone staying here could suddenly have an accident or develop a terminal illness. Use plenty of metal windchimes and make sure you do NOT have fire energy i.e. a bright lamp or crystal lights here or there a grave misfortune could occur.

When the Mountain Star 2 combines with the Water Star 6, it indicates a life of ease and leisure. This auspicious combination however will be instantly ruined if a 5 rod windchime is placed here. If this happens, the trinity of tien ti ren unfortunately gets activated in a negative way. The presence of windchimes here will also attract wandering spirits causing disturbance to the family.

When Mountain Star 2 combines with Water Star 7 the luck of children will not be good. Anyone living here will have problems conceiving children. In fact in this current Period of 8, everything about this combination is bad. A good remedy is to use water to subdue the 7.

When the Mountain Star combines with the Water Star 8, use water to overcome the bad health star. But otherwise richness and wealth comes to you. The problem with ill health is minor and is easily remedied. When the Mountain Star 2 combines with Water Star 9 there is extreme bad luck. Nothing can succeed unless you place lots of plants in this part of the house. Water plants are better.

147 MOUNTAIN STAR 3 COMBINATIONS

Whten the Mountain Star is 3, it brings aggravations and plenty of ill tempers. Those affected will become difficult to live with and since the Mountain Star stands for relationships and the number 3 brings problematic relationships, it is truly a very harmful indication. The placement of cures is definitely a must and this has to be done according to what the accompanying water star is.

When it combines with the Water Star 1, wealth luck is indicated. However, do note that the Mountain Star 3 is dangerous since this is the hostile star. Combined with the 1 Water Star however, relationships get soothed. Use water to enhance this combination further. Note that prosperity luck is good but if you do not have the karma/luck to enjoy wealth luck, your own bad temper will spoil everything for you.

When the Mountain Star 3 combines with the 2 Water Star, it is a bad indication and can get dangerous for those in politics. Residents have a tendency to obesity. Some masters recommend the presence of gold and fire as remedies for loss of power and authority.

When the Mountain Star 3 combines with the 4 Water Star, there is a real danger of mental instability, plenty of headaches and aggravations. Residents will feel really stressed out. The best cure is to turn on bright lights in this corner.

When the Mountain Star 3 combines with the 5 Water Star there is loss of wealth and severe cash flow problems. If your bedroom is here, financial loss will be very dramatic. If the kitchen is here, sickness is inevitable. Better not to stay in this part of the house. Exhaust the 5 with metal chi, but do not use windchimes or bells as this aggravates the number 3 star. Use a copper mountain painting instead to suppress the bad chi.

When the Mountain Star 3 combines with the 6 Water Star it suggest that any growth coming your way will slow, held up by the hostile Mountain star.

When the Mountain Star 3 combines with the 7 Water Star, you run the risk of getting robbed or burgled. When the Mountain Star 3 combines with the 8 Water Star it is not a good indication for children under 12 years. The solution is to install bright lights where this combination occurs.

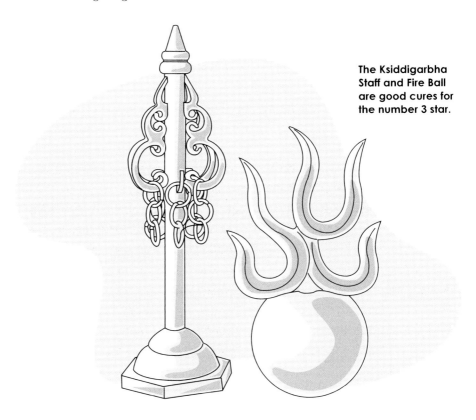

The Ksiddigarbha Staff and Fire Ball are good cures for the number 3 star.

MOUNTAIN STAR 4 COMBINATIONS

It is useful to know that the mountain star is especially influential in the current Period of 8 as this is the number that signifies the mountain. When you live in a part of the house where the mountain star is 4, the luck of love relationships can be in overdrive – manifesting in a wonderful romance or leading to some excess, especially when matched with a strong water star.

When the Mountain Star 4 combines with the Water Star 1, romance luck is indicated, but too much water can lead to illicit love affairs that result in sordid scandals. You need to ensure there are no water features such as a pond or an aquarium in the sector. If there is unhappiness related to relationships, problems can result – here using plants to weaken the water and strengthen the wood of 4 is a good idea.

When the Mountain Star 4 combines with the Water Star 2, it often indicates some kind of illness involving the internal organs hitting the matriarch. If the master bedroom is located here, it suggests that the husband could get involved in a love affair outside the marriage. And when the Mountain Star 4 combines with the Water Star 3, there could be emotional stress due to aggravating relationship problems. The best cure for both situations is to use red or fire energy to subdue the strength of the wood element. A bright light here will work wonders.

When the Mountain Star 4 combines with the Water Star 5 residents staying here could be prone to sexually transmitted diseases and there is also some danger of the matriarch contracting breast cancer. If the Water Star is 6, the indication is bad luck for women staying here as they will have to bear a heavy family burden. If the Water Star is 7, anyone staying here will go through some severe bad luck in love as they could well get cheated by someone they love, especially someone of the opposite sex.

When the Mountain Star 4 combines with the Water Star 8 it brings danger to very young children staying here especially newborn babies. For adults however ,the indication is auspicious. Finally, when the Water Star is 9, it indicates good fortune for those preparing for life i.e. for the younger generation getting ready to start a career. It indicates good fortune for those still studying at school or college.

The number 4 star indicates luck in relationships and a pair of mandarin ducks is a good enhancer for this star.

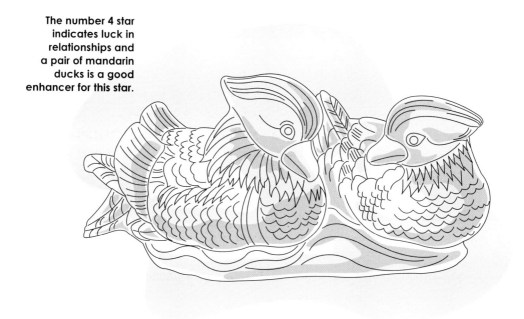

149 MOUNTAIN STAR 5 COMBINATIONS

When you live in a part of the house where the Mountain Star is 5, misfortune is likely to hit, as the five yellow is an afflictive star. Here the impact is on your relationships and on your health luck and you will definitely need metal element energy to help subdue this star.

When the Mountain Star is five and the Water Star is 1, residents staying here will be vulnerable to sex-related misfortunes and could also succumb to hearing problems. When the Water Star is 2, the misfortune luck is quite heavy indeed. The extreme bad luck could even lead to serious illness, which can turn out to be fatal. The best cures for this combination would be all metal windchimes especially those that can also create the sound of metal on metal, so they should be hung in places that catch the wind.

When the Mountain Star is 5 and the Water Star is 3, residents will experience plenty of money troubles. There is always shortage of cash and worse, continuous disputes with each other and with others over money. There is also very bad business luck. In this instance, the best cure is the staff and ball of Ksiddhigarbha made of metal or even better, a statue of Ksiddhigarbha himself. When the Water Star is 4 or 5, it is just as bad or even worse!

When the Water Star is 6, luck is better as finances are in better shape, but when the Water Star is 7, then problems are once again indicated. Here the residents will meet up with the fortune of having their wealth stolen from them. There are also problems caused by excessive gossiping. There is danger to the mouth – either poisoning or too much talking.

When the Mountain Star is 5 and the Water Star is 8, the lucky star is still not strong enough to suppress the effect of the *wu wang* and illness problems related to the limbs, joints and bones of the body are indicated. Residents must be careful when indulging in sports such as mountain climbing, skiing and so forth. When the Water Star is 9, there is also bad luck and tempers will fray. Excessive mental disorder or stress leads to unhappiness and dissatisfaction.

So do note that a Mountain Star 5 is a misfortune indication. The best remedy is to create metal energy in the sector.

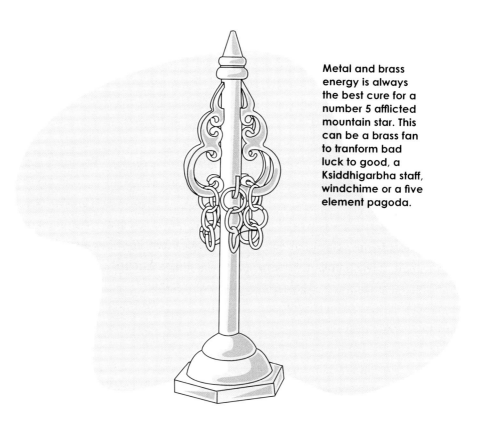

Metal and brass energy is always the best cure for a number 5 afflicted mountain star. This can be a brass fan to tranform bad luck to good, a Ksiddhigarbha staff, windchime or a five element pagoda.

150 MOUNTAIN STAR 6 COMBINATIONS

This is a lucky mountain star and although the strength of the number 6 is not at its zenith in Period 8, it can still create the foundation for a good water star to bring excellent rewards and wealth luck. So if you live in a part of the house where the mountain star is 6, you can be reasonably sure that the indications will not be too stressful.

When the Water Star here is 1, it becomes a Ho Tu Combination, bringing good fortune. There is wonderful financial luck and the family will produce many high achievers who bring honor to the family. You can enhance this with lots of metal energy. Residents living here also benefit from wearing gold.

When the Water Star is 2 there is great affluence and everything is easily successful. It is not even necessary to enhance any further unless you wish to place a beautiful liu li vase filled with faux diamonds or ingots. When the Water Star is 3, there will be plenty of unexpected windfall luck that bring financial gain. Residents are also never short of speculative luck so they can indulge in some small time gambling. Fortune smiles on them. Enhance the sector with a blue tortoise or a three legged toad. When the Water Star is 4, it will be the women of the household that benefit from an unexpected windfall. Activate this luck the same way.

When the Mountain Star is 6 and the Water Star is 5, luck is not great and finances are not in very good shape. Here the Water Star 5 needs to be suppressed with metal energy and it is advisable to use the transformational metal fan. This should blow away any bad luck affecting your finances. When the Water Star is 7, you can get cheated of your money as there is "sword fighting" bad energy.

You might have to say goodbye to your money as chances of getting it back are less than nil. If you stay here, the best thing to do is to move out of the room as it is tough to install cures here.

If the Water Star is 8, the luck is amazingly good. There is wealth, popularity, prosperity as well as great richness. This is probably the best combination in Flying Star in any sector, better even than the double 8. When the Water star is 9, windfall luck is magnified.

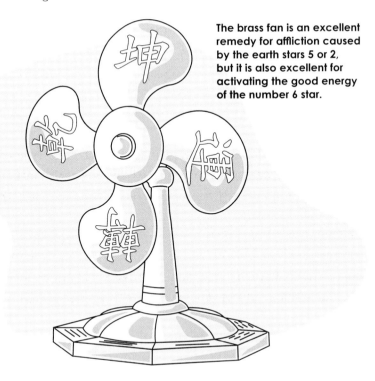

The brass fan is an excellent remedy for affliction caused by the earth stars 5 or 2, but it is also excellent for activating the good energy of the number 6 star.

151 MOUNTAIN STAR 7 COMBINATIONS

When the Mountain Star is 7, the luck of the sector is seriously afflicted. In the current Period of 8, the number 7 indicates betrayal and loss with a suggestion of hostility involved.

When the Water Star in the sector is 1, the combination spells prosperity luck brought by the auspicious water star, but there is danger of it being stolen or lost, so there is a need to be careful. Subdue the 7 and enhance the 1 with a water feature here.

When the Water Star here is 2, money luck gets dissipated and stolen from residents often without them even knowing. Their employees will rob those in business. Children luck is also seriously dimmed, so couples staying in such a bedroom have a hard time conceiving.

When the Water Star is 3, there is serious danger of injury to the limbs. Residents should be very careful. Placing red here is a definite help. When the Water Star is 4, the residents here are easily fooled by conmen, and in matters of the heart, they can be easily taken for a ride by someone of the opposite sex.

When the Water Star is 5, residents will have their wealth stolen from them. There are also problems caused by excessive gossiping. There is danger to the mouth, either poisoning or too much talking. If you are up for an inheritance, you could lose it all unless you move out of this sector of the house.

When the Water Star is 6, you are likely to be cheated of your money and the "sword fighting" bad energy causes you serious problems. The good thing however is that you have excellent speculative luck and you will come through Ok, but nevertheless it is still aggravating and you might want to consider moving out of this room.

When the Water Star is also 7, then there is serious bad luck as we have now entered the Period of 8. The best way to suppress the energy of 7 is by having a water feature here but you can use this only if this is not your bedroom, as water in the bedroom brings bad luck too. If it is your front or back door that has this double 7, then yours is likely to be a Period 7 house and I strongly advise you to change your house into a Period 8 house.

When the Water Star is 8, your wealth luck is excellent, and when the Water star is 9, there are extreme problems all through the Period of 8. Troubles are caused through excessive vulnerability to sexual advances. There is also danger of fire hazards as your prosperity luck attracts greedy and jealous eyes!

The brass rhino is excellent for keeping the #7 star under control.

152 MOUNTAIN STAR 8 COMBINATIONS

When the Mountain Star is 8, the luck of the sector is excellent, bringing incredible happiness and health luck to the residents of the family. In the Period of 8, the mountain star 8 is either at the front or the back of the house, and this means its good fortune luck directly benefits the household. .

When the Mountain Star is 8 and the Water Star is 1, luck is excellent with the combination of these two auspicious white numbers. Everything is very promising as there is money as well as family luck. Relationships in the family bring contentment and joyousness. You can if you want to enhance the Water Star with water and the Mountain Star with crystals.

When the Water Star is 2, many feng shui masters are in agreement that this is even better than a Water star 1, as the sum of ten formed here is particularly auspicious. You should enhance with a water feature to actualize the wealth luck and there is definitely plenty of that. If the Water Star is 3 however, there is danger to young children and it is advisable to move them from here. But wealth luck stays excellent, as the combination here is a Ho Tu combination. When the Water Star is 4, there will be a very overpowering matriarch. So any mothers-in-law staying here should be moved to another room. The love life of the younger generation can also suffer from an interfering mother if the mother of the house lives here.

When the Water Star is 5, the lucky Mountain Star is not strong enough to suppress the effect of the *wu wang* and illness problems related to the limbs, joints and bones of the body are indicated. Residents must be careful when indulging in sports like mountain climbing, skiing and so forth. When the Water Star is 6, there is everything - wealth, popularity, prosperity.

When the Water Star is 8, this combines with the Mountain Star to form the double 8 and then of course we have two superlative stars! In the Period of 8, there are four houses that have the occurrence of the double 8 either at the front of the house or at the back. Although the double 8 effect is however not as good as the 8/6 or 6/8 because it is hard to activate both excellent mountain and excellent water, nevertheless, rooms located here do enjoy excellent wealth and relationship luck. And when the Water Star is 9, it indicates excellent current and future prosperity luck.

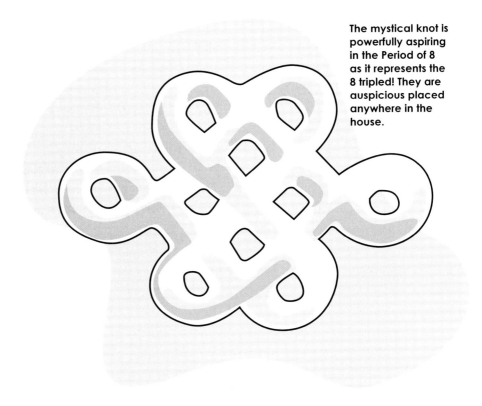

The mystical knot is powerfully aspiring in the Period of 8 as it represents the 8 tripled! They are auspicious placed anywhere in the house.

153

MOUNTAIN STAR 9 COMBINATIONS

When the Mountain Star is 9, the luck of future prosperity is strong. Here the fire element of the number 9 also enhances the Earth energy of the mountain, so the effect of the 9 is auspicious in the long term and the good fortune may not be immediately felt.

Combined with a Water Star 1, the effect is a sum of ten situation, which overrides the fire and water combination. Here water and fire bring mutual benefits, but there can also be hidden danger, so there is a need to be careful. This is a combination that is luckier in period 9 than in the current period. Better to activate the Water Star 1. This combination signifies balance of yin and yang, but it also indicates more sons than daughters if your bedroom is here. If the master bedroom is here, the wife tends to be the dominant one in the marriage.

When the Water Star here is 2 and the Mountain Star is 9, health luck gets seriously weakened. If you stay in a room with this combination, you succumb easily to health problems. But there is good family luck with lots of children and grandchildren. In a good period such as the current Period of 8, the family will produce many outstanding scholars. The fire energy here must never be allowed to get dim as this causes the good luck to dissipate.

When the Water Star is 3, there will be all kinds of misunderstandings amongst family members, although these seldom lead to severe quarrels. The fire energy of 9 helps reduce the severity of the quarrelsome vibes brought in by the number 3. There will be rebellious sons, although one amongst them will make the family proud. He will bring honor and wealth to the family.

When the Water Star is 4, we see a Ho Tu combination that is very auspicious. There is completion luck and also a great deal of recognition in your life. Promotions in your job and fame in your work come easily. In the current period of 8, this combination paves the way for a great deal of recognition luck in the future. This combination brings more luck to the wife than the husband, although beware, too much water can bring a sex scandal!

When the Water Star is 5, residents will suffer from financial loss over a long period of time. This is a sad combination, which must be suppressed with metal energy. Problems arise incessantly and there seems no end to all the problems. There could be abortion or even a death. The patriarch here will be very stubborn and succumb to bouts of severe temper tantrums almost resembling a mental disorder. This is a very dangerous combination and you must use metal to suppress.

When the Water Star is 6, it can bring some good fortune to the patriarch, but in the longer term, it is unfavorable both to the patriarch of the house as well as to the father-in-law. Grandsons of the family can also suffer. There is the danger of disobedient sons clashing with the older folk. Here we are seeing a "fire at heavens gate" combination. This can bring illness, loss and financial damage. As long as only a single family unit live here, the luck is fine, but if this is a family home with several generations living under the same roof, this combination is to be feared.

When the Water Star is 7, the men of the family tend to become alcoholic or get involved in serious gambling. This happens when the combination hits the master bedroom. Residents appear affable at the start, but they tend to get ugly in the end, so their business and social connections get ruined. If this is the bedroom of a young lady, she will lose her husband or boyfriend. Better to find another room or the young girl gets cheated and only has heartbreak to look forward to.

When the Water Star is 8, you have a great abundance of wealth luck, which also lasts and lasts. It is a very favourable combination which sees the combination of purple with white. The only danger here is that the woman in this sector tends to become very aggressive, while the men here tend to become weak. There could be a lot of negative fireworks between husband and wife – plenty of quarrels.

But this indicates also a family that can get super rich with plenty of good properties and profitable businesses. Those under the influence of this combination have much to look forward to and young men and women hoping to find themselves a good spouse will be able to do so. There is much happiness luck indicated.

When the water star is 9, it signifies the double 9 which brings a smooth life with few or no obstacles. The double 9 occurs in period of 9 houses and it signifies plenty of excellent good fortune. However it also indicates more daughters than sons.

154

THE FRONT & BACK OF THE HOUSE

THE FACING PALACE

The most important part of any house in terms of getting the flying star right is what we term the *facing palace*. Generally speaking, this is the sector of the house where the main door is located i.e. it is the front central grid of the flying star chart. Sometimes it may not be where the main door is located because the facing palace could be on another side of the house facing a beautiful view overlooking a valley. In such a case, the facing palace is at once at a disadvantage simply because without a main door there, it doesn't get activated. When there is a door in the facing palace, each time people move in and out of the house, the palace is activated, and if there are auspicious numbers there, the potential for good fortune is so much stronger.

Sometimes there may be a door in the facing palace but the door may be facing a different direction from the house orientation. This is fine as long as the flying star chart was drawn up based on the house facing direction and NOT the door facing direction.

There are many "specials" that refer directly to the facing palace under advanced feng shui readings. Many of these specials require the presence of water near the vicinity of the facing palace as one of the best ways of energizing this important palace of the home.

Water feng shui is a specialized field of study, but for now, just take note that water must be on the left hand side of the main front door. This means looking out, the water should be on the left. This guideline holds true irrespective of whether the water is inside or outside the house. Note that water placed on the right creates the cause for the man of the house to fall prey to predatory females outside the marriage.

THE SITTING PALACE

This is an equally important palace as the numbers in this sector also reflect the overall energy of the home. The sitting palace is the sector of the house where generally the back door is located i.e. it is the back central grid of the flying star chart.

The sitting palace defines the support feng shui of the house and it is generally expected for there to be slightly higher ground here. If there is a mountain behind, it indicates there is support and protection for the home. In the current period of 8, the mountain and water stars 8 are located either in the facing or sitting palaces only. They are not found anywhere else in the home. As such, both the facing and sitting palaces become extremely prominent in terms of defining the feng shui energies of the home.

Ideally the mountain star 8 should be at the back in the sitting palace, and the water star 8 should be at the front in the facing palace. This is described as "ideal mountain, ideal water" and houses with this kind of chi energy enjoy the potential of having the best kind of feng shui chart, best in that it is easier to activate and easier to get the feng shui right.

If there is higher ground behind, it signifies the mountain, and as with water features, you should have some kind of opening – a door or a window here to enable the mountain energy to enter into the home.

155

IMPORTANT PARTS OF THE HOME

THE MASTER BEDROOM

An important palace is where the master bedroom is located. It is worthwhile to make a special effort to sleep where the most auspicious mountain and/or water stars have flown into. If you must choose between two bedrooms, always choose one that has an auspicious water or mountain star; which can be the water or mountain star 8 in the current period.

There is no need to activate with water in the bedroom and it is not advisable to do so. Usually, bedrooms are placed on the upper levels of homes so it is sufficient to activate the ground level where the water or mountain 8 occurs. If you cannot get the water star 8 room, then select other auspicious white stars. Number 1 should be the second choice while 6 is third. This is because 6 is a tired old star in period 7 – but 6 is much better than the dangerous 5s or 2s.

THE HEART OF THE HOME

The heart of the home is the center and the numbers that fly here are usually read as having a powerful effect on the feng shui experience of the entire house, especially if the center of the home is a large spacious room. The general rule is to that where the star numbers are auspicious or lucky the center of the home should be a large room that houses an important area of the house. This can be the living room, dining room or bedroom.

If the heart of the home is host to bad luck numbers however, then their influence should be reduced as much as possible by reducing the space here.

LOCKING UP MISFORTUNE STARS

A novel but effective method of overcoming the pernicious influence of bad stars such as the 5s, the 2s and the 3s is to literally lock them up inside specially constructed "cells". You can use a store room to imprison troublesome stars so the household does not feel their malevolence. The store room does not need to be large. But there should be a door and the room should be kept locked and undisturbed. This means having a small room in the heart of the home. This is one of the more effective ways of taking care of the powerful *wu wang* (five yellow) misfortune star.

EXPANDING AUSPICIOUS STARS

On the other hand, when the center water and mountain stars are auspicious such as when the number 9 flies in either as water or mountain star in PERIOD 8 HOUSES e.g. houses that have a facing direction of Northwest or Southeast, then the feng shui thing to do would be to knock down the walls that imprison these auspicious stars. An open hall concept would be a smart thing to do since this in effect spreads the auspicious influence to the rest of the house. Good fortune chi then gets distributed to a greater floor area of the house.

156

SELECTING PERSONAL SPACE

SELECTING ROOMS BASED ON KUA NUMBERS

Residents bring their own intrinsic chi to the rooms they occupy and this is always defined by their KUA numbers. The formula for obtaining one's KUA numbers based on the Eight Mansions school of feng shui has been covered earlier. From the KUA number can be derived your self element as well as your self number, which can now be used in conjunction with Flying Star to select the most auspicious room for you. According to the traditional texts, all of us exert our own chi presence – and when our personal chi harmonizes with that of the room we occupy, good fortune will abound.

Check if the mountain star or water star empowers and produces your KUA number.

For instance, if your KUA number is 2, you belong to earth element. If the room you occupy has a 7 mountain star, you will see instantly that the metal of 7 will exhaust the earth of 2. So you will forever feel tired and tense. But if your live in a room with the 8 mountain star, then it adds earth energy to you, thereby strengthening your good fortune.

If a KUA 2 person lived in a room with the 5/9 combination of stars, then even though the 5/9 is not a desirable combination, nevertheless, the harmony between 5 and 2 (both being earth numbers) and between 2 and 9 (here the fire of 9 produces the earth of 2) makes this an excellent room for the KUA 2 person.

So the clever way to apply this small but important guideline is to see how your KUA element interacts with the respective elements of the water and mountain stars. If the water star element produces your KUA element, then obviously money luck for you will be excellent. And if the mountain star element produces your element, then your popularity, health and social life will be most fortunate.

In the same way if the water star number element destroys your KUA element sleeping there will cause you to lose money. If it is the mountain star number that destroys your KUA number element, then sleeping in that palace will cause you to lose power, authority and influence.

157

SUPERIMPOSING THE CHART

When you are have thoroughly familiarized yourself with the flying star charts, annual and monthly charts, the next crucial step in practicing this method of feng shui is to transfer the chart numbers of the different sectors onto the actual spaces of your home.

The most efficient way of doing this is to use a floor plan of the house and to then superimpose the flying star chart onto the plan using the compass directions as a rough guide.

There is some disagreement regarding how charts should be transferred onto the floor plan. Practitioners in Hong Kong use the PIE CHART method in that they actually superimpose the circular compass onto the floor plan and subdivide your house space according to the compass demarcations of directions. This is similar to a pie chart.

A second method of superimposing the chart is to use the Lo Shu grid of nine squares to place the numbers onto the floor space. This appears to be the more logical way to do it and I prefer to use the nine sector grid method myself. However, here some practitioners feel that the entire Lo Shu grid chart should be superimposed onto the floor plan equally while others are of the opinion that the numbers of each grid should be placed into the different rooms based on compass directions and the way the walls of the house have been erected.

I use this last method to transfer the flying star numbers onto the floor plan. Using the compass to identify the sectors I take note of walls that have already been built to make my flying star readings. Using this method, some rooms being smaller than others mean certain set of numbers (comprising water and mountain stars) will exert a greater influence than other numbers. I feel that the walls of any building do create a natural demarcation of the flying star grids. This also offers greater accuracy in determining the energy of the home.

SUPERIMPOSING THE FLYING STAR CHART

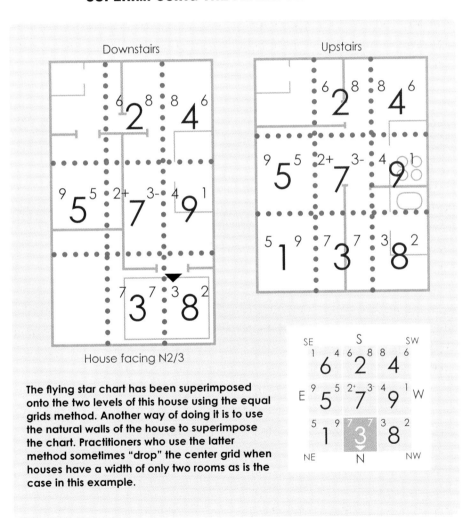

House facing N2/3

The flying star chart has been superimposed onto the two levels of this house using the equal grids method. Another way of doing it is to use the natural walls of the house to superimpose the chart. Practitioners who use the latter method sometimes "drop" the center grid when houses have a width of only two rooms as is the case in this example.

158

SMALL AND BIG TAI CHI

One of the most important guidelines of practicing Flying Star feng shui is that all feng shui charts — be they period charts or annual or monthly charts - can be superimposed onto the whole house, or they can be superimposed onto individual rooms. This follows the concept of big Tai Chi or small Tai chi. This is the yin and yang symbol and it refers to the space we wish to feng shui.

Not many people realize this, but in planning our feng shui, we demarcate the space and it is up to us where we wish to create the parameters of space to include into our investigation.

Usually we refer to the whole house as the big Tai Chi of our space. Here we consider the whole house as our Universe and we superimpose the Flying Star chart onto the whole house using compass directions to give us our reference points for anchoring the relevant numbers. This enables us to make an overall reading of the flying star energy of the home.

In addition, we can also look at each individual room as a microcosm of space as well, so that the same chart can be also superimposed onto individual rooms. Here we will place the numbers of the flying star chart onto different corners of the room using compass directions to guide us as to which set of numbers goes where. Doing this enables us to know which corners are lucky and which have unlucky numbers.

This is the Small Tai Chi usage of the flying star chart. Flying star charts can therefore be used to demarcate energies based on either big or small tai Chi. Knowing this principle means we also know that the auspicious stars of water and mountain can be "activated" for the whole house as well as for individual rooms.

159 CHART OVER THE WHOLE HOUSE

It is very important to superimpose the chart over the whole house as a first step to deciphering the flying star numbers and investigating what they are telling us about the different corners and sectors of the house. And since houses have layouts and rooms the best way of applying Flying Star is to identify rooms of the house and label them according to their compass directions.

Thus, for instance, we should try to determine in which compass sector the main door into the house is located and then we determine the relevant flying star numbers from the chart that apply to that compass sector. For example if the main door is located in the South sector then we look at the set of numbers − comprising Period Star, Water Star and Mountain Star − that is in the South sector.

In the same manner, we determine the relevant set of numbers for the dining room, living room, kitchen as well as main bedrooms in the home. Superimposing the numbers onto the home in this way takes account of both the compass directions as well as the layout of the house. This method of using the charts gives weight to the way the rooms of the house have been laid out.

Obviously we would want to ensure that the best stars i.e. the auspicious water and mountain stars are captured in the sectors which house the important rooms of the house, such as the master bedroom, as well as the facing palace where the main entrance door is located, as well as the sitting palace where probably the back door is located.

Superimposing the chart over the whole house gives the practitioner a snapshot of the quality of energies in every corner of the house, thereby making it easy to activate the sectors with lucky stars and to suppress whatever afflictions may have been revealed via the unlucky stars.

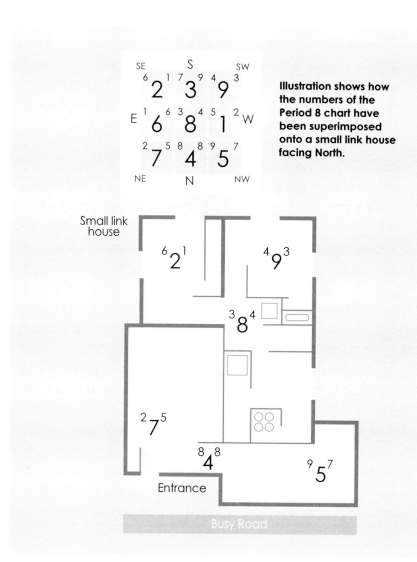

Illustration shows how the numbers of the Period 8 chart have been superimposed onto a small link house facing North.

160 FLYING STAR FOR APARTMENTS

I f you live in a high-rise apartment or condominium, you need to make sure that you are using the correct flying star chart for your home. The general rule is to assess the compass orientation of the entire apartment building and use the facing direction of the whole building to determine the correct flying star chart that is to be superimposed onto individual apartments.

Thus if the whole apartment building faces South 3, then it is the flying star chart facing S3 that is then used to determine the flying star energies of your apartment. The numbers in this chart are then superimposed onto your apartment floor plan using the real orientation of your apartment to guide you. Thus if the master bedroom of your apartment is in the East sector of your apartment, then you look for the set of numbers placed in the East sector of the relevant chart – then depending on whether the Water Star and Mountain Star is lucky or not you can then determine if the master bedroom has lucky stars. In the same way, you can determine the luck of other rooms in the apartment as well as also the luck of its facing palace.

Here the individual apartments of the whole building are viewed as the "Small Tai Chi" of the building.

Generally, this method of superimposing the flying star numbers apply to apartments that go up to the ninth level. Those apartments that are higher than the ninth floor, however, are deemed to be separate units of dwellings and for these apartments, the facing direction that determines the correct flying star chart does not depend on the facing direction of the whole building. Instead, here, the facing direction would be the facing direction looking out from the largest picture window or if there is a balcony, from the balcony. Hence looking out from the apartment you determine the facing direction from the largest opening (can be a window or a sliding door) and this will determine the chart that applies to the apartment. Once you have determined the correct chart you can undertake the analysis and place the remedies and enhancers accordingly.

161 CHART OVER INDIVIDUAL ROOMS

You can treat individual rooms in large houses in exactly the same way that you treat individual apartment units in low rise apartment buildings – using the Small Tai Chi approach. Hence it is possible to superimpose the entire nine grid flying star chart into each of the rooms separately. This then reveals the luck of the different compass sectors of the room and doing this helps you to arrange your furniture to benefit the residents of the household. Beds and sofa chairs can be placed towards the corners of rooms that are lucky. Similarly the unlucky or afflicted sectors can then be avoided OR cures can be placed into corners that are negatively affected.

Using the Pa Kua which shows the eight compass directions to represent the flying star chart this is shown in the illustration overleaf. Note that this application of the small tai chi of space applies to all the compass methods of feng shui. The different charts that are drawn up based on the compass can always be superimposed onto individual rooms as well as onto the entire abode for purposes of deciphering the distribution of luck in houses according to the dynamics of space and time.

SUPERIMPOSING PA KUA ONTO INDIVIDUAL ROOMS WITHIN THE HOUSE

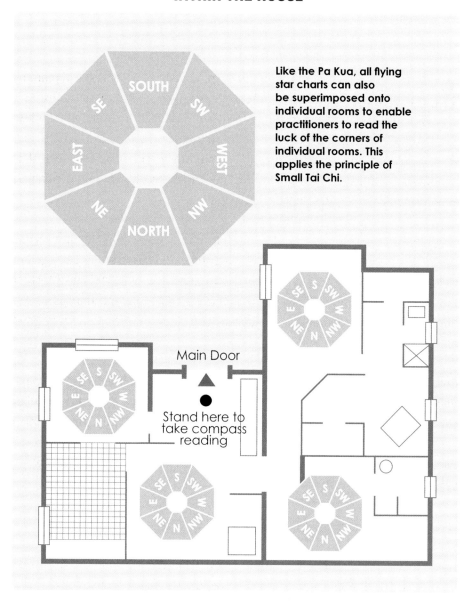

Like the Pa Kua, all flying star charts can also be superimposed onto individual rooms to enable practitioners to read the luck of the corners of individual rooms. This applies the principle of Small Tai Chi.

Main Door

Stand here to take compass reading

24 MOUNTAINS ANNUAL UPDATES

Now that you are well versed with Flying Star and the annual and monthly changes of energies that affect everyone's feng shui, there is just one final thing to investigate and these are annual "luck stars" that fly into each of the 24 mountains each new year. Incorporating these "luck stars" into your annual updating exercise fine tunes your practice of Flying Star feng shui considerably. These stars affect houses based on their sitting directions bringing good or bad energy to residents.

The best source for identifying the "annual 24 mountain stars" is the Chinese Tung Shu, a compilation of astrological and feng shui calculations put together by learned masters of the science from Hong Kong, Taiwan and China. Much of this data is usually given in raw form using classical language and a knowledge of old style Chinese metaphors is needed to understand the nuances of good and bad stars.

Collectively these are referred to as the "annual luck stars of the 24 mountains" and they affect houses and people alike. Amongst these "stars" are the Tai Sui or Grand Duke Jupiter, the "King of the Luck stars", and also the Three Killings which we have already discussed, as they are annual afflictions that must be factored into annual updates. However, while these two stars make an appearance every year, there are other stars that do not.

Usually we turn to the Tung Shu to obtain a list of these "other stars" at the start of each new year. Understanding their meanings however requires one to have knowledge of feng shui jargon in the Chinese language. Do keep track of these lucky and unlucky stars and make sure you factor them into your feng shui updating program at the start of each year. These indicate the good and troublesome months of houses and also indicate the nuances of luck during each twelve months of the year. Special advice for residents are also sometimes offered wherever relevant.

Thus the practice of Flying Star is a dynamic activity. Ensuring a continuity of good feng shui requires us to keep track of changing energies from year to year. For these and additional information required to update your feng shui each year, visit www.wofs.com at the start of each new year. The 24 mountain luck stars and annual and monthly flying star charts are regularly posted and freely available at the website.

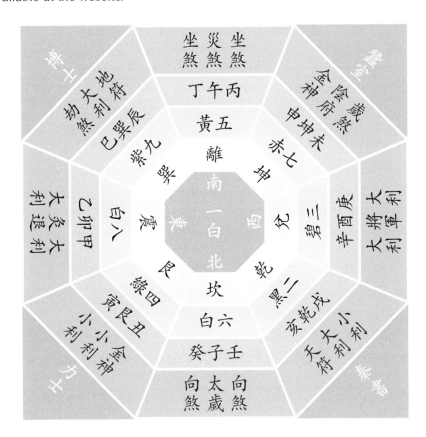